THE BOOK
OF
IRISH BULL

Des MacHale

Better than all the udders

ᙏERCIER PRESS

Mercier Press
P.O. Box 5, 5 French Church Street
16 Hume Steet, Dublin 2

© Des MacHale, 1987

A CIP record for this title is available from the British Library

ISBN 0 85342 822 0

12 11 10 9 8 7 6 5 4

This book is affectionately dedicated to
Herb and Barbara Cummings
of the Workshop Library on World Humour, Washington, D.C.
who inspired the foundation of
The Irish Bull Library of Humour at University College, Cork.

Printed in Ireland by Colour Books Ltd.

CONTENTS

INTRODUCTION

The dictionary defines an IRISH BULL as 'an expression containing a contradiction in terms or implying a ludicrous inconsistency in speech frequently unperceived by the speaker,' and if you're still with me after that mouthful and if you'll pardon the expression, that's nothing but a load of pure Bull. The Irish Bull is nothing more than the way we speak in Ireland, the way our peculiar minds express themselves, our thoughts and words tripping over each other in a relatively recent and alien tongue. To the unsubtle listener, the Irish Bull may indeed sound like a contradiction when taken literally, but the philosopher.will realise that at times it contains and conveys a deep truth.

This book contains what is possibly the greatest collection of Irish Bulls ever assembled in one volume. Very many of them are genuine, as any visitor to Ireland will verify, and we see many of them through the eyes of the prototype Irishman and Irishwoman, Pat and Bridget, who first made their appearance in my *Irish Love and Marriage Jokes*. Pat is frequently joined by his friend Mike to form the pair who together spawned a million Pat and Mike jokes in the United States around the turn of the century.

The Irish Bull is possibly the only art form where the definition of the art form is itself an example of the art form — here is the best definition of an Irish Bull:
'If there were twelve Irish cows lying down in a field and one of them was standing up, then that one would be an Irish Bull.'

Sir John Mahaffy defined an Irish Bull as a bull that is always pregnant. You'd need AI to sort that one out!

Finally, even this book itself is an Irish Bull - it had a gestation period of ten years.

I

FOR WHOM THE BULL TOLLS – DEATH

The Irish are one of the few nations who are capable of dying laughing – in fact it might be claimed that we invented the concept of the jovial wake or the dead man's last party. A very large proportion of Irish Bulls concern death or dying and the reason may be that the language of the living suddenly becomes hilarious when used in relation to death.

* * *

Pat and Mike were passing a cemetery.
'What's that Pat?' asked Mike.
'That's a cemetery, Mike,' said Pat, 'that's where all the dead people live.'

* * *

Pat's next-door neighbour had died and was lying in his coffin with a great big smile on his face.
'Why is he smiling?' Pat asked the man's widow.
'Well it's like this,' said the widow, 'he died in his sleep and he doesn't know he's dead yet. He's dreaming he's still alive, and what I'm afraid of is that when he wakes up and finds out he's dead, the shock will kill him.'

* * *

If Brian Boru hadn't gone to his tent to pray, the chances are he'd still be alive to-day.

* * *

Mike once explained the increasing death rate in the country as follows – 'sure there's people dying this year who never died before.'

* * *

When Bridget died she stipulated no floral tributes as she was allergic to flowers.

* * *

Pat was talking with the local undertaker who told him that business had never been worse — he hadn't buried a living soul for over six months.

*   *   *

Pat was attending a neighbour's funeral, a man who when alive had not suffered fools gladly.
'Do you know what I'm going to tell you,' he said to Mike, 'if that man was alive to-day he would turn in his grave to see some of the people who came to his funeral.'

*   *   *

Mike was delivering the graveside oration for an old friend of his who was being buried.
'That man in the coffin,' he thundered, 'is a living proof of the fact that hard work never killed anyone.'

*   *   *

'I see where King Leopold of Spain has died,' Pat informed Bridget one night.
'Is that a fact, Pat?' said Bridget, 'I never knew that man was alive until I heard he was dead.'

*   *   *

'You can't escape fate,' Mike used to say, 'show me a place where people don't die and I'll go and end my days there.'

*   *   *

Pat's wife Bridget made him promise that he would have her coffin opened three days after her death to make sure she hadn't been buried alive.

*   *   *

The following toast was drunk to King George IV on his visit to his loyal subjects in Dublin:—
MAY GEORGE THE FOURTH FOR EVER EVER REIGN
AND NEVER NEVER DIE
AND AFTERWARDS MAY GEORGE THE FIFTH
REIGN TWICE AS LONG AS HE.

*   *   *

The postman called at Pat's house one morning with a letter edged in black.

'Not bad news, I hope,' said the postman.

'I'm afraid it may be,' said Pat. 'It looks like a letter telling me that my brother Jim has died in America. I'd recognise his handwriting anywhere.'

*　*　*

I'd hate to die and be buried in Siberia,' said Bridget to Pat one cold night as she snuggled up to him in bed, 'it's so cold there I'd freeze to death.'

*　*　*

Pat and Mike were at a friend's funeral and were remarking on the number of people who were there.

'Look at the hypocrisy of this crowd,' said Pat, 'none of them would have come to the funeral if he was alive.'

*　*　*

When Bridget's father died she went to the undertakers to buy a shroud.

'How much are the shrouds?' she asked the man behind the counter.

'Ten pounds, madam,' he replied.

'Ten pounds!' she said in disgust, 'I can get one for five pounds down town.'

'Those are of inferior quality madam,' said the man, 'the corpse would have his knees out through it in a week.'

*　*　*

Mike's uncle Tom was lucky. He was sentenced to death by hanging but saved his life by dying in prison.

*　*　*

'A stone coffin,' Pat used to say, 'is a great invention, because it would last a man a lifetime.'

*　*　*

Pat and Mike were watching the wall being built around the new graveyard.

'Progress is a great thing and cannot be halted Mike,' said Pat, 'that's the graveyard I hope to be buried in, if the good Lord spares me.'

*   *   *

When the posh new hearse arrived in the village, Bridget said she was dying to get into it.

*   *   *

'Is your father long dead?' Mike asked Pat.

'Well,' said Pat, 'if he had lived until next Saturday, he would have been dead a month last Tuesday.'

*   *   *

When a well-known politician died suddenly, Pat remarked, 'It was typical of the man to die unexpectedly.'

*   *   *

Pat was in a fit of depression and one night Bridget came home to find him standing on a chair with a rope around his waist.

'What the hell are you doing?' she asked him.

'I'm committing suicide,' replied Pat.

'Then why haven't you got the rope around your neck?'

'Well I had,' said Pat, 'but it was choking me.'

*   *   *

Mike went to the doctor with a bad gash on the top of his head.

'How did you get that?' the doctor asked him.

'Actually,' said Mike, 'I bit myself.'

'But you couldn't have,' said the doctor, 'it's too high up.'

'I stood on a chair,' said Mike.

*   *   *

'I hear they did a postmortem on your father,' a neighbour said to Bridget.

'Yes,' said Bridget, 'but unfortunately not until after he was dead, otherwise it might have saved his life.'

* * *

An undertaker was in the neighbourhood to collect a client but by mistake knocked on Pat's door.

'Can I help you sir?' asked Pat.

'I hope so,' said the undertaker, 'is this where the man that's dead lives?'

* * *

Pat once attended a public hanging. As the condemned man began to climb the rickety stairs leading to the gallows, he asked, 'Are these stairs safe?'

* * *

Pat and Mike were in an accident while out driving. As they lay stunned on the roadside, Pat said to Mike, 'Talk to me Mike, is it alive or dead you are?'

'Neither of them,' said Mike, 'I'm merely struck speechless.'

* * *

Pat and Bridget were once involved in a motor accident and Bridget lay sprawled across the back seat roaring with pain. 'Be quiet,' said Pat, 'you'd think there was nobody killed except yourself.'

* * *

Pat's father was being treated by the doctor for years for gout but just as the treatment had taken effect he died of a heart attack. The doctor consoled his widow by saying 'at least you have the consolation of knowing he died fully cured.'

* * *

11

In a fit of depression, Mike once threatened to commit suicide or perish in the attempt.

* * *

Bridget and all her family were strong Catholics. She used to say that she would rather die than be buried in a Protestant graveyard.

* * *

As Pat was watching his late uncle, a man of some five feet, being fitted into his coffin, he remarked to the undertaker that the coffin was a bit big.
'Don't worry,' said the undertaker, 'he'll soon grow into it.'

* * *

Pat owned an antique shop and among the most expensive items on sale were two skulls, a big skull and a little skull. The big skull was a skull of Brian Boru as a man and the little skull was a skull of Brian Boru as a boy. Each skull was accompanied by a certificate, signed by Brian Boru himself, verifying that the skulls were genuine.

* * *

Pat was in the army but ran away in the heat of battle and was charged with desertion. At his trial he defended himself by saying, 'I'd prefer to be a coward for five minutes than a corpse for the rest of my life.'

* * *

When Bridget's brother was missing at sea, presumed drowned, she was asked to give a description in order to help with the identification of the body if and when it turned up. All she could remember was that he spoke with a pronounced stutter.

* * *

Pat went to the undertaker to inquire about the cost of a funeral. When told the figure he said to the undertaker, 'That's more than £500 up on last year.'
'I know,' said the undertaker, 'but you must remember that the cost of living is going up all the time.'

* * *

Pat's cousin had made his own coffin in his work shop. 'That's very presumptious of you,' said Pat to him, 'how do you know you will ever live to use it?'

* * *

A friend of Pat's, one of a pair of identical twins, had just died. Pat went along to sympathise with the surviving twin and said to him, 'I'm sorry for your troubles, tell me, was it you or your brother that died?'

* * *

The following advertisement for coffins was placed in an Irish provincial newspaper:
NOBODY HAVING ONCE TRIED ONE OF OUR COFFINS WILL EVER USE ANY OTHER.

* * *

Bridget looked up from her newspaper one evening and asked Pat, 'what are posthumous works Pat? It says here that the posthumous works of this author are selling very well.'
Pat smiled indulgently at his wife's ignorance.
'Posthumous works, Bridget,' he told her, 'are works a man writes after he's dead.'

* * *

Two old Irish proverbs —
MAY YOU LIVE TO EAT THE CHICKEN THAT SCRATCHES OVER YOUR GRAVE.

MAY YOU NEVER SEE YOUR WIFE A WIDOW.

* * *

'Wasn't it very sad about Frank O'Sullivan,' said Pat to Mike one day.
'What happened to him?' asked Mike.
'He died in hospital,' said Pat, 'after an unsuccessful suicide attempt.'

* * *

Pat's grandfather was found guilty of sheepstealing, but got away with a suspended sentence — he was hanged. However, the execution had to be postponed for several weeks because he produced a doctor's certificate stating that he was too ill to be hanged and could not be moved from his cell without imminent danger to his health.

* * *

'Did your husband die easy?' Bridget asked a recently widowed neighbour.
'Indeed he did not,' she replied, 'it nearly killed poor Seán to die.'

* * *

Pat was talking to a young clerical student who hoped to be ordained as a priest in a few years time.
'I hope,' said Pat, 'that I may live to hear you preach my funeral sermon.'

* * *

'I've heard that the town's oldest resident is dead,' said Bridget to Pat one evening.
'I've heard that fellow's death reported so often and found the reports to be false that I won't believe it unless I hear it from his own lips,' replied Pat.

* * *

Watching a line of condemned criminals waiting in the rain to be hanged, Mike remarked, 'I hope the hangman hurries up and does the job because those poor fellows will catch their death of cold.'

* * *

Space was becoming limited in the old graveyard and Pat was afraid that when his time came there would be no place for him to rest his bones. After a bit of thought he sent the following suggestion to the local authorities — confine burials in the graveyard to those living in the parish.

* * *

Mike was on a very stormy sea voyage and feeling very seasick.
'Don't worry,' said the captain, 'you'll live.'
'Don't say that,' said Mike, 'it's only the thought of dying that's keeping me alive.'

* * *

When Pat was feeling very depressed he was asked if he had ever contemplated suicide.
'Never,' he replied, 'it only ruins your health.'

* * *

The great philosopher Hegel is said to have perpetrated the following Irish Bull on his deathbed:—
'Only one man ever understood me perfectly — and he didn't really understand me.'

* * *

The following is taken from an account of a funeral in an Irish provincial newspaper: —
By the graveside, Mr. Pat Murphy, a nephew of the deceased, had the misfortune to fall and break his leg. This naturally threw a gloom over the entire proceedings.

* * *

The following sad little example of a perfect Irish Bull is taken from the *Cork Constitution* in 1858.
The coroner's verdict was that the baby was found dead in a closet, having been born alive but never breathed, and that it died immediately afterwards for want of proper assistance at the time of its birth.

* * *

Mike is dead   against all those flashy new hearses. He is on record as saying that he wouldn't be seen dead in one of them.

* * *

Bridget was once feeling so ill she declared,'If only I could drop dead now I'd be the happiest woman alive.'

* * *

The following is a genuine extract from an obituary notice published in an Irish newspaper:
    We regret to announce the death of Mr. Patrick
    O'Flaherty, the well-known secret agent.

* * *

The same paper carried the following *in memoriam* notice in its columns:
    In loving memory of Sam O'Hara who died ten years
    ago today. Inserted by his wife Mary.
            Safe in the arms of Jesus.
    You'd be alive to-day if you did what I told you.

* * *

Pat's son was a chronic medical student. One evening he came home and announced proudly to his father, 'after all those years practising on models, at last they've given me a real live corpse to work on.'

* * *

Pat and Mike were walking in a graveyard when they saw a tombstone which read:
        IN LOVING MEMORY OF DAN O'HARA
            WHO DIED IN AMERICA
'That's funny,' said Pat, 'I could have sworn that Dan O'Hara died before he went to America.'

* * *

Bridget was walking in a cemetery one day when she saw a tombstone inscribed with the words

I STILL LIVE

She said to herself, 'if I was dead at least I'd be honest enough to own up to it.'

* * *

Mike decided that he would be cremated because he heard that undertakers were charging the earth for burials.

* * *

Pat, however, was dead against cremation. He was afraid that the crematorium might catch fire and everybody would be burned to death.

* * *

A man in Bridget's village had been ill from heart disease for many years. Finally, he caught a chill and died within a few days.

'At least,' Bridget consoled his widow, 'he didn't die of anything serious.'

* * *

Pat died and Bridget claimed it was the most expensive funeral ever held. She made the mistake of burying him in a £50 a week hired dress suit.

* * *

Pat was lying in his coffin and a neighbour remarked on how well he looked.

'So he should,' said Bridget, 'he was jogging ten miles a day.'

* * *

EPITAPHS

Here lies the body of Thomas Murphy
who was lost at sea and never found
had he lived he would have been buried here.

*   *   *

This stone was erected to the memory of Din Joe O'Connell who was drowned in the Lakes of Killarney by a few of his dearest friends.

*   *   *

In loving memory of John O'Donoghue who was fatally burned by an explosion of a lamp filled with Murphy's non-explosive burning fluid.

*   *   *

Here lies the body of Lt. Col. MacMahon, accidently shot by his batman while cleaning his rifle. Well done thou good and faithful servant.

*   *   *

Erected to the memory of John Buckley, accidently shot as a mark of affection by his brother.

*   *   *

Here lies the body of James Shaw who came to Mullingar and died for the benefit of his health.

*   *   *

2

MOVABULL – TRANSPORTS OF DELIGHT – MOBULL

The Irish have always been a wandering people, so naturally they have a great interest in transport and loco-motion. The time element involved in moving from place to place gives rise to a great number of bulls. As any foreign industrialist knows, the Irish have a healthy contempt for timetables, schedules and deadlines, and once again the static nature of language is not capable of coping with these rapidly changing situations.

* * *

Pat was late for work one morning, so the excuse he gave to the boss was that the train was late.
'Next time the train is late,' said the boss, 'come on the earlier train.'

* * *

Pat and Bridget went on a round-the-world cruise last year. Next year they hope to go somewhere else.

* * *

Mike went into the big city and was looking for a shop in which to buy a pair of braces.
'Where is the braces shop sir please?' he asked a passerby.
'On the other side of the street,' he was told, so he crossed the road and addressed himself to a policeman.
'Excuse me sir,' said Mike, 'where is the other side of the street?'
'It's over there,' said the policeman, pointing across the street.
'That's funny,' said Mike, 'I was over there and someone told me it was over here.'

* * *

Pat once got a job as a deep sea diver. One day he got the following message on his headphones — come up immediately, we're sinking.

* * *

When Mike was working with the railways he was heard to make the following announcements.

THE TEN O'CLOCK TRAIN LEFT AT HALF-NINE AND THERE WILL BE NO LAST TRAIN TO-NIGHT. THE REAR PORTION OF THE TRAIN WILL NOT RUN TO-NIGHT.
THIS TRAIN STOPS NOWHERE.

When asked by a woman when was the next train for Dublin leaving, Pat replied, 'the next train for Dublin has just left.'

* * *

Mike was once offered a free round-the-world trip but he refused it because he had no way of getting back.

* * *

Pat was insuring his car against fire and the insurance agent asked him if he would like to insure it against theft as well. 'Don't be daft,' said Pat, 'nobody would ever steal a burning car.'

* * *

Pat and Mike were driving along a narrow country road with a cartload of hay when a tourist came driving around the corner and, unable to avoid them, he ploughed through the hedge into the hayfield where the car exploded into a ball of flames.

'Bejapers,' said Pat to Mike, 'some of those tourists are terrible drivers, we only just got out of that field in time.'

* * *

Pat had just arrived in England and wanted to send a telegram to inform Bridget that he had got there safely.

'How much for a telegram?' he asked the clerk.

'£5 for the telegram,' said the clerk, 'and £5 for delivery.'

'I'll just pay for the telegram,' said Pat, 'and I'll save on the delivery charge by sending her a letter telling her to come and collect the telegram.'

* * *

Pat met Mike in the big city one afternoon.

'Did you go home yet?' asked Pat.

'No,' said Mike, 'did you?'

* * *

Pat was walking home one evening carrying a large sheet of glass when a policeman began to eye him suspiciously.

'Where did you get that?' he asked.

'I found it,' said Pat, 'it fell off the back of a lorry.'

* * *

Sign seen on a Cork street (no joking!):

THIS STREET IS A ONE WAY CUL-DE-SAC AT BOTH ENDS.

* * *

Mike was arrested one night while driving his car at over a hundred miles an hour. He gave the following explanation to the judge – 'I was hurrying home so that I wouldn't be arrested for speeding.'

* * *

When the new fire engine arrived in the village, the Council were looking for suggestions as to what might be done with the old engine.

'Why not,' suggested Pat, 'keep the old one for false alarms?'

* * *

On his way to America by boat, Pat was feeling more than a little seasick. He went straight to the engine room and delivered the following ultimatum to the crew – 'either stop this ship to steady it a bit or I'm getting out to walk.'

* * *

Pat and Bridget were shopping in a big store when they became separated. Bridget went to the information desk and asked the girl there if she had seen a man wandering around without a woman looking like her.

* * *

Pat and Bridget were on a holiday in theTropics and on their first night there there was a violent storm.
'I didn't sleep a single wink last night with all that thunder,' confessed Bridget the next morning.
'Why didn't you wake me?' said Pat, 'you know I can't sleep when there's thunder.'

* * *

Bridget got a puncture but consoled herself that at least it was only flat on the bottom.

* * *

Mike had the following advice for motorists on narrow country roads – the best way to pass a herd of cows on the road is to keep behind them.

* * *

Pat was on a long train journey and he nipped off the train to have a quick drink. He looked up suddenly to see the train chugging out of the station, so he ran down the track shouting furiously, 'come back, come back, you've got a passenger on board that's left behind.'

* * *

Mike attended the Galway Races and heard the following announcement:—

> The Galway Plate will be run on Friday; however if it's raining on Friday, the race will be run on Thursday.

* * *

Pat and Mike were on a long country walk and were getting a bit tired.
'How far is it back to town?' they asked an old man leaning over a fence.
'Ten miles exactly,' said the man.
'Great,' said Pat to Mike, 'that's just five miles each.'

* * *

'How far is it to town?' a tourist asked Bridget.
'It's a good distance,' she replied, 'If you were going to walk, you would have to take a bus.'

* * *

'How far is it to town?' a tourist on a walking trip asked Pat.
'About ten miles,' answered Pat.
Seeing the tourist's face fall, Mike said, 'Make it five Pat. Can't you see he's walking.'

* * **

Bridget was reading about a terrible air crash in Spain in which all the passangers were killed
'That's terrible,' she commented, 'there is nothing worse than being killed on your holidays.'

* * *

Bridget was in the big city travelling by bus and wasn't too sure where she should get off.

'Where's the stop for the Zoo?' she asked a woman sitting beside her on the bus.

'Watch me,' said the woman, 'and get off three stops before I do.'

* * *

Pat went to the filling station and told the lad there to put ten gallons of petrol in his tank. After a few minutes the lad came round to the front of the car and said to him, 'I'm afraid it will only hold nine and a half gallons. Would you like to drive round for a few minutes so that I can fit the other half gallon in?'

* * *

Mike was not a great traveller. As he said himself, he only went to London once and then he only got as far as Dublin.

* * *

There was a crash on the old single line West Clare Railway and Pat was reading the official regulations to see what the legal position was. At last he found the relevant paragraph and it read as follows:—

If two trains approach each other on the same track then neither shall proceed until the other has got off the track and given way to it.

* * *

Speaking of the West Clare Railway, one of its trains was described as —

the most punctual train in Ireland and a great source of inconvenience to the travelling public.

* * *

Pat and Bridget once travelled to Dublin to see the invisible man.

* * *

When motor horns were first introduced, Mike commented that the only people who paid any attention to them were dogs.

* * *

Pat was asking a young lad who lived near him how many miles he cycled to school.
'Ten miles a day sir,' answered the lad, 'five miles to school and five miles home again.'
'That's a lot of cycling,' commented Pat, 'six schooldays in the week, so that's sixty miles a week. No, hold on, Saturday is only a half day, so it's only fifty-five miles in all — a bit better than I thought.'

* * *

Mike once got a job as cabin boy on a ship and as the ship was about to sail the captain asked him to go below and fetch a jar of beer.
'No I will not,' said Mike, 'If I did that the ship might sail without me.'

* * *

Pat was explaining to his employer why he was so late for work.
'The bus I came in,' he told him, 'was full so I had to walk.'

* * *

Bridget once took up jogging and attempted to run around the Phoenix Park. About three-quarters of the way around, however, she got tired and thought she wouldn't make it, so she jogged back again.

* * *

Pat was driving in his car when he glanced at the petrol guage and saw that it registered empty. 'This can't be good for the car,' he said, 'driving around with no petrol.'

* * *

Driving home one night, Pat noticed that he seemed to have very little petrol left in his tank so he accelerated a bit so as to get home before he ran out of petrol.

* * *

Pat and Bridget were once flying home from London when their plane caught fire. Bridget became hysterical but Pat comforted her by saying, 'don't worry, girl, the fire isn't in our half of the plane.'

* * *

Pat and Mike were once climbing a big mountain but about halfway up they became very tired and thirsty. 'I'll tell you what,' said Pat, 'let's go down to that pub at the bottom, and we can climb the other half tomorrow.'

* * *

One of the wheels had fallen off Pat's car while he was driving along the highway and he was charged with careless driving. He offered the following excuse to the judge.

When I tightened the wheel nuts before, I tightened them too tight, so when I went to tighten them again, I thought that if I didn't tighten them so tight, they wouldn't be too tight, but I must have tightened them too loose.

* * *

Pat was travelling by train when he realised that that particular train did not stop at his little home town. So he called one of the ticket checkers on the train and asked him, 'could we stop long enough for me to run home and tell Bridget I'm being carried through?'

* * *

An Irish petrol company once made the following announcement:

> If all the other petrol companies stopped giving free gifts, we would be the first to stop. As it is, we must reluctantly continue.

* * *

Mike once got a job driving a snowplough but refused to take it out because the weather was so bad.

* * *

Pat was working on the railway line when suddenly a train came speeding towards him along the track. He took off down the line but of course he was knocked down by the train and badly injured. When he woke up in hospital, his friend Mike asked him why he hadn't run up the bank at the side of the track.
'Don't be a fool,' said Pat, 'if I couldn't beat it on the flat, what chance had I running up a slope?'

* * *

Pat and Mike arrived in Majorca on a holiday.
'Did you travel here by sea or air?' a hotel porter asked them.
'I don't know,' said Pat, 'my wife bought the tickets.'

* * *

Old Irish cure for sea sickness — sit under a tree.

* * *

Pat was boasting about the new Rolls-Royce he had bought.
'When the engine is running at full throttle,' he declared, 'the only sound you can hear is complete silence.'

* * *

Mike travelled to London but was disgusted to find that nobody there had ever heard of him.
'Why back in Ireland,' he exclaimed, 'I'm world famous.'

* * *

Pat and Bridget were flying to England by aeroplane because they felt it was the only way to fly.

'Does this plane travel faster than sound?' Bridget asked the hostess.

'No, madam,' replied the hostess, 'it doesn't.'

'I'm glad,' said Bridget, 'because I want to talk to Pat during the journey.'

*   *   *

Mike's son decided to hitchhike to Dublin, so he got up and made an early start to avoid all the traffic.

*   *   *

Pat and Bridget went on their holidays to Barcelona where they saw a genuine Spanish Bull.

'What's the matter dear?' Pat asked Bridget.

'Look at that notice in our bedroom,' laughed Bridget, it says:

> 'PLEASE DO NOT STEAL TOWELS
> IF YOU ARE PERSON NOT TO DO THIS
> PLEASE NOT TO READ NOTICE'

*   *   *

Irish Railway announcement: 'There will be no trains running between Limerick and Mallow on Sunday next and delays of up to thirty minutes can be expected.'

*   *   *

Pat and Mike were out boating when their boat sprang a large leak. Immediately, Pat punched another hole in the boat saying, 'This will let it out.'

All the time Mike was smiling because it wasn't leaking at his end of the boat.

*   *   *

Mike was involved in a motor accident and was asked to fill in an insurance claim. He wrote as follows:

'Coming home I drove up the driveway of the wrong house and collided with a wall I haven't got.'

* * *

A Visual Irish Bull —
An Irish self-righting canoe.

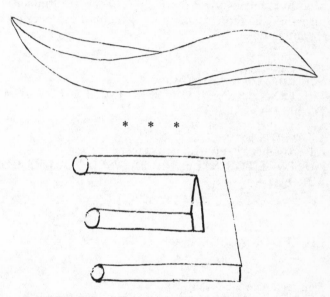

* * *

THE IRISH BULL ELECTRIC PROD

3

BULLETINS – NOTICES AND HEADLINES

There is something about notices, headlines, telegrams and the like that naturally gives rise to ludicrous Bulls. The language is condensed, perhaps too condensed at times, and inevitably ambiguity arises. The phenomenon is a world wide one, but as usual the Irish examples are funnier, more ingenious and more ludicrous, all the more so because they are authentic.

*　　*　　*

Notice in a confectioner's shop:
THE PENNY BUNS HAVE BEEN INCREASED FROM 10p TO 20p

*　　*　　*

Advertisement in an Irish newspaper:
PASSPORT FOR SALE, NEVER USED. OWNER GOING ABROAD

*　　*　　*

Sign on an Irish shop:
CLOSED ON ACCOUNT OF RE-OPENING

*　　*　　*

Sign seen near a convent:
THESE GROUNDS ARE PRIVATE. TRESPASSERS WILL BE PROSECUTED WITH THE FULLEST RIGOUR OF THE LAW
SIGNED
THE SISTERS OF MERCY

*　　*　　*

Sign in an optician's window:
IF YOU CAN'T SEE THIS NOTICE COME INSIDE AT
ONCE – YOU MAY NEED SPECTACLES

* * *

Road sign seen near Killarney:
THIS IS THE WRONG ROAD TO DUBLIN
DO NOT TAKE THIS ROAD

* * *

Many Irish dance halls display the following sign over the
exit:
ENTRANCE OUT

* * *

A post office had for many years a postbox displaying the
following notice:
FOR LETTERS TOO LATE FOR THE NEXT DELIVERY

* * *

Sign seen on a barber's window:
OUR HAIR RESTORER IS SO POWERFUL – THE LESS
YOU USE OF IT THE BETTER IT IS

* * *

Notice on a Cork shop door:
GONE TO LUNCH – BACK IN AN HOUR.
ALREADY GONE HALF AN HOUR

* * *

Sign in a Leinster shop:
VISIT OUR BARGAIN BASEMENT ON THE THIRD
FLOOR

* * *

Notice on the road leading into Castlebar:
WELCOME TO CASTLEBAR
EARLY CLOSING DAY ALL DAY THURSDAY

* * *

Notice in a shop:
DON'T BE CHEATED ELSEWHERE – COME IN HERE

* * *

An old Irish shebeen according to Carleton is reputed to have
displayed the following notice:
NO CREDIT GIVEN BARRING TO THEM WHO PRODUCE
READY MONEY

* * *

Sign in an undertaker's:
OUR COFFINS HAVE A LIFETIME GUARANTEE

* * *

Notice in an optician's window:
IF YOU CAN'T SEE, YOU'VE COME TO THE RIGHT
PLACE

* * *

Notice in a psychiatric hospital:
WE'RE ALL HERE BECAUSE WE'RE NOT ALL THERE

* * *

Sign seen in a home laundry:
WHY KILL YOURSELF WITH WASHING?
LET US DO IT BY HAND

* * *

Notice reported in a beauty shop:
EARS PIERCED WHILE YOU WAIT
PAY FOR TWO AND GET ONE DONE FREE

* * *

The following notice stood for many years on the banks of the River Shannon:
WHEN THIS NOTICE IS UNDER WATER IT IS UNSAFE TO CROSS THE RIVER AT THIS POINT

*　*　*

Notice in a post office:
TO PREVENT PENS FROM BEING STOLEN, NO PENS WILL BE PROVIDED

*　*　*

Sign seen at a country race meeting:
DONKEY RACES OPEN TO RESIDENTS OF THE PARISH ONLY

*　*　*

Notice seen on a shop:
YES WE ARE OPEN – PLEASE CALL BACK AT SOME OTHER TIME

*　*　*

Newspaper headline:
BODY OF MAN FOUND IN GRAVEYARD

*　*　*

Newspaper advertisement:
GENUINE ANTIQUES FOR SALE – AS NEW

*　*　*

Notice on tip head:
NO DUMPING ALLOWED BY ORDER

*　*　*

Newspaper advertisement:
FOR SALE SECOND HAND COFFIN, HARDLY EVER USED, ONE CAREFUL OWNER

*　*　*

Newspaper headline:
MAN STATED TO BE CRITICAL FOLLOWING FATAL ACCIDENT

* * *

Notice on the old West Clare Railway:
NO OVERTAKING ON THIS LINE

* * *

Newspaper headline:
POPE DIES FOR SECOND TIME IN A MONTH

* * *

Sign on an Irish garage:
LAST PETROL STATION UNTIL THE NEXT ONE

* * *

The following notice was displayed for many years on a jail:

ALL PRISONERS NOT BACK IN JAIL BY 11 p.m. SHARP WILL BE LOCKED OUT FOR THE NIGHT

* * *

Newspaper headline in 1986 (absolutely genuine!)
PRICELESS IRISH CHALICE WORTH £5.5M

* * *

Sign in an Irish auctioneer's:
THE HIGHEST BIDDER TO BE THE PURCHASER
– UNLESS SOMEBODY BIDS MORE

* * *

Notice in a shop:
NO DISSATISFIED CUSTOMER IS EVER ALLOWED TO LEAVE THIS SHOP

* * *

Newspaper headline:
PASSENGERS HIT BY CANCELLED TRAINS

* * *

Notice in a Restaurant:
CUSTOMERS WHO THINK OUR WAITRESSES ARE
RUDE SHOULD SEE THE MANAGER

* * *

Notice on a Connaught dance hall:
DISCO ON SUNDAY NIGHT VERY EXCLUSIVE
EVERYBODY WELCOME

* * *

Notice in a cemetery:
YOU ARE ALLOWED TO PICK FLOWERS ONLY OFF
YOUR OWN GRAVE

* * *

Notice outside an undertaker's:
PARKING FOR CLIENTS ONLY

* * *

Notice on a Dublin shop:
OPEN 24 HOURS A DAY
LONGER AT WEEKENDS

* * *

Notice in a chemist shop:
WE DISPENSE WITH ACCURACY

* * *

Notice beneath a Calvary scene in a graveyard:
EXECUTED BY O'SULLIVAN BROTHERS

* * *

Notice in a hotel:
PLEASE DO NOT SWITCH ON TELEVISION EXCEPT
WHEN IN USE

*   *   *

Newspaper small ad:
HEARSE FOR SALE; RECONDITIONED ENGINE,
ORIGINAL BODY

*   *   *

Notice on a drinks dispenser machine:
THIS MACHINE IS PERMANENTLY OUT OF ORDER

*   *   *

Notice in a golf club:
TROUSERS MAY NOW BE WORN BY LADIES ON THE
COURSE — BUT THEY MUST BE REMOVED BEFORE
ENTERING THE CLUBHOUSE

*   *   *

Sign in a post office:
PENS WILL NOT BE PROVIDED UNTIL PEOPLE STOP
TAKING THEM AWAY

*   *   *

Sign in a barber shop:
SPECIAL OFFER: HAIRCUTS 50p ALL THIS WEEK
ONE PER CUSTOMER ONLY

*   *   *

Sign on a church:
CLOSED ON SUNDAYS

*   *   *

Notice on a restaurant:
SORRY — WE ARE CLOSED FOR LUNCH

*   *   *

Sign on a Connaught dance hall:
LADIES AND GENTLEMEN WELCOME REGARDLESS OF SEX

*   *   *

Inscription on a box of string:
FOR BITS OF STRING TOO SHORT TO BE OF ANY USE

*   *   *

Notice on a Midland hotel:
DRIVE-IN SWIMMING POOL.

*   *   *

Notice on a lorry:
DRINK T AND P MINERAL WATERS

*   *   *

Notice in a Cork fashion shop:
OUR BIKINIS ARE SIMPLY TOPS

*   *   *

Notice on a grocer's shop:
CLOSED FOR LUNCH UNLESS YOU WANT SOMETHING

*   *   *

Sign on a Dublin Supermarket
NO SMOKING – GUIDE DOGS EXCEPTED

*   *   *

4

EDIBULL AND DRINKABULL – FOOD AND LIQUOR

The Irish are renowned for their drinking habits throughout the world – but they only drink to forget the fact that they are alcoholics. In between drinks they are also known to eat from time to time, though an Irishman will never eat on an empty stomach. In general, he likes to combine both activities by drinking a certain potent black beverage because 'there's eatin and drinkin in it.'

*   *   *

Bridget keeps hoping that some day scientists will find a cure for wheatgerm.

*   *   *

When Mike ate fish he always ate herrings. 'Herrings are the freshest of all fish,' he used to declare, 'because the herring lives longer after it's dead than any other creature.'

*   *   *

Pat walked into a bar and asked for a whiskey and ice.
'I'm sorry sir,' said the barman, 'we have no ice.'
'I'll have a whiskey and water then,' said Pat.
'Sorry sir,' said the barman, 'all our water is frozen.'

*   *   *

'Let's go to McCarthy's Restaurant,' said Pat to Bridget one evening.
'No,' said Bridget, 'let's go somewhere else. That place is so crowded, no one goes there any longer.'

*   *   *

Pat and Mike went picking blackberries.
'How will I know the ones that are ripe?' Mike asked.
'That's easy,' said Pat, 'the blackberry is the only fruit that's red when it's green.'

*   *   *

Bridget was asked to describe what it was like when Pat had one of his massive hangovers.

'Well', she said, 'the morning after, I bring him up the newspaper and he reads the obituary column. Then, if he's not in it, he gets up.'

* * *

Mike and his friends went into a pub and found a nice quiet corner. Mike went over to the bar and ordered twenty pints of beer.

'Would you like a tray, sir?' asked the barman.

'Certainly not,' said Mike, 'haven't I enough to carry with all these drinks?'

* * *

Pat was describing how crowded his local pub was one night. 'First of all,' he claimed, 'I couldn't get in for the crowd, and getting out was even worse.'

* * *

Mike was out on a drinking spree one night and left his umbrella behind in one of the pubs he visited. Next day he called to nine of the pubs and failed to find his umbrella, but in the tenth one it turned up.

'Do you know what I'm going to tell you,' he said to the barman over a celebratory pint, 'you're the only honest barman in town. All the others said they hadn't got it.'

* * *

Pat didn't really have a drink problem. He took a lifelong pledge to abstain from all alcohol when he was eighteen and every three months for forty years afterwards.

* * *

The Irish Pioneer Total Abstinence Association has a curious rule that its members may consume alcohol in the form of sherry trifle, porter cake, and brandy flavoured chocolates. As Bridget put it, 'you can eat drink, but you can't drink drink.'

* * *

'Just how drunk were you?' the judge asked Mike, after a policeman had given evidence that Mike had refused to walk a white line without a safety net.

'I was as drunk as a judge,' said Mike.

'Surely you mean as drunk as a lord,' said the judge.

'Yes, my lord,' said Mike.

'Look,' said the judge, 'stop fooling about, how drunk were you?'

'I was sober enough to know I was drunk,' said Mike.

Helplessly, the judge asked the policeman to continue his evidence on Mike's condition.

'He was speechless drunk, your honour,' said the policemen, 'and using foul, obscene and insulting language.'

* * *

During the dreadful famine of 1846, a relief worker was bringing food to a starving family in a remote Irish village.

'Thank God for the famine,' said one old man, 'if it wasn't for it, sure we'd all starve to death.'

* * *

'Why are you eating so fast?' Bridget once asked one of her little children.

'I want to finish my meal,' said the little lad, 'before I lose my appetite.'

* * *

Pat once opened a bakery shop. He used to sell a bread so light that a pound of it weighed only twelve ounces.

* * *

Old Irish Proverb—
He that is drunk and knows he is drunk is sober;
but he that is drunk and thinks he is sober is really drunk.

* * *

'Irish literature,' said Mike, 'was largely written by people who never drew a sober breath after the age of seven'.

* * *

A beggarperson once called at Bridget's door and told her that he had just sold his last saucepan in order to buy some porridge to cook in it.

* * *

Pat was once describing a recipe for Bridget's soup.
'She takes a pint of water,' he said, 'and boils it down to make it strong.'

* * *

Bridget was getting a bit fed up because for three days in a row the milk had gone sour, yet she didn't want to offend the milkman by mentioning the fact.
'If I were you,' said Pat, 'I'd take the bull by the horns and demand fresh milk.'

* * *

Mike was explaining to his wife why the meat he had just bought from the butcher didn't taste very good.
'It comes from cattle that are killed after they died,' he explained.

* * *

Advertisement in an Irish Newspaper:
For sale, a quantity of port drunk by Queen Victoria on her visit to Dublin.

* * *

Pat once bought a cow from a man because he told him that it would give milk indefinitely without having a calf. 'It's in her blood,' he assured him, 'because she came of a cow that never had a calf.'

* * *

Pat and Mike were once the worse for drink.
'Do you remember your man Frank Murphy?' asked Pat.
'What's his name again?' asked Mike.
'Who?' asked Pat.

* * *

Bridget once left the following note for the milkman:
Two pints of milk to-day. By to-day I mean tomorrow as I wrote this yesterday.

* * *

Mike came home from the pub one night to find his house empty and all the doors locked. Finally he broke in through a window and found the following note from his wife on the table:
Your salad is in the oven and you'll find the key of the door under the mat.

* * *

'I don't like this cheese with all the holes in it,' said Pat to Bridget over tea one evening.
'Well,' said Bridget, 'eat the cheese and leave all the holes on the side of your plate.'

* * *

Pat went into the illicit liquor business making illegal poteen. When he took his stuff into town to sell he always drove his donkey cart very slowly. It wasn't because he was afraid of the police – he just wanted to give it a chance to age a bit.

* * *

Bridget awoke one night to hear Pat moving quietly about the bedroom.
'What are you looking for?' she asked him.
'Nothing,' he replied, 'nothing at all.'
'Then you'll find it,' she told him, 'in the bottle where the whiskey used to be.'

* * *

Mike was staying in a little country hotel and was wandering about early in the morning. The landlord said to him, 'I'm sorry sir the bar won't be open for another hour, but would you like a drink while you're waiting?'

* * *

Pat and Bridget went into a cafe for breakfast but were disgusted with the small portions they received.

'Look at this bit of bacon,' complained Pat to the waitress, 'it's not enough for a man's breakfast if he died in the night.'

* * *

Bridget was put on a severe diet but her doctor was amazed to see her in a restaurant tucking into bacon, cabbage and potatoes.

'What about your diet, Bridget?' he asked her.

'Oh, I've had my diet,' said Bridget, 'now I'm having my dinner'.

* * *

Mike was asked what was his favourite drink.

'The next one,' he replied.

* * *

Pat and Mike were staying in a hotel a bit the worse for drink. They fused all the lights in the hotel playing a game. The object of the game was to turn out the light quickly enough so they could see what the dark looked like.

* * *

Bridget once left the following note for the milkman:

Dear milkman,

No milk to-day.

If this note blows away, please knock.

* * *

5

INCURABULL – MEDICINE AND THE BODY

Pat's father used to follow the medical profession – he was an undertaker. Most Irishmen and Irishwomen believe that what doctors preach is a load of bull anyway and that anyone who has the energy to visit a doctor isn't really ill in the first place. As for psychiatrists, it was that honorary Irishman, Sam Goldwyn, who first coined the immortal phrase 'anyone who goes to see a psychiatrist should have his head examined.'

An Irishman's body has wittily been defined as 'merely a machine for turning potatoes into human nature' and it doesn't take too much imagination to come up with a liquid equivalent.

* * *

Mike once discharged himself from a psychiatric hospital. 'They would drive you mad in there,' he declared.

* * *

Pat had no faith at all in doctors. He complained to his friend Mike, 'the last time I was ill, the doctor stuffed me so full of drugs, pills and tablets that I was sick a month after I was well.'

* * *

Bridget once went to the doctor and complained of insomnia. He advised her to go home and sleep it off.

* * *

The following is an extract from a first-aid manual published by the Mercier Press : –
Keep administering the kiss of life until the patient is dead.

* * *

Mike once went into hospital to have his legs amputated but the surgeon assured him he would have him back on his feet in no time.

* * *

When Bridget was a nurse, one of her principal tasks was waking up patients to give them their sleeping pills.

* * *

'Learn to cut your fingernails with your left hand,' Pat's father used to advise him, 'in case you lose your right hand.'

* * *

Mike had a large bald patch so he used to wear a wig with a large bald patch on the top. He figured that that way nobody would realise he was wearing a wig.

* * *

Pat and Bridget's dentist used to boast that he spared no pains to satisfy his patients.

* * *

Pat was telling Mike that when he was born he weighed only a few ounces.
'Wow,' said Mike, 'that's almost incredible, tell me, did you live?'
'Live?' chuckled Pat, 'boy, you ought to see me now.'

* * *

Bridget was once being examined by her optician.
'Now shut your eyes,' he told her, 'and look at me.'

* * *

Pat was once prescribed an emetic by his doctor, but, try as he liked, he couldn't keep it in his stomach.

* * *

Mike used to boast that he had an uncle so small that he had to stand on a box just to blow his nose.

* * *

Pat was explaining to Mike how nature sometimes compensates for deficiencies of the body.

'For example,' he told him, 'if someone has weak eyesight, he may have good hearing to compensate for his deficiency, or if he has poor hearing, he may have a good sense of smell.'

'I think I see what you're getting at,' said Mike at last, 'I've often noticed myself that if a fellow has one short leg, the other one is always a little bit longer.' (Possibly the best of all Irish Bulls).

*   *   *

Pat was warned about the smells coming from his drains so he wrote to the local council asking them to come and investigate.

The council officer replied that there was no point in doing this as it was the smell you couldn't smell at all that did you the most harm.

*   *   *

Bridget used to be a haemophiliac but finally cured herself by acupuncture.

*   *   *

Mike went to the doctor who gave him some pills to take. 'Are these habit forming?' Mike asked him.

'Certainly not,' said the doctor, 'I've been taking them myself every day for the last twenty years and I can assure you they are not habit forming.'

*   *   *

Pat went to the doctor who prescribed suppositories. When he returned a few weeks later the doctor asked him if the treatment had worked.

'Not a bit,' said Pat, 'I ate about a dozen of them and for all the good they did me I might as well have stuck them in my rear end.'

*   *   *

Pat was once at death's door but the doctor pulled him through.

* * *

Bridget was asked to compose a bidding prayer for the medical profession at a religious service.
She prayed, 'Lord, grant patience to our doctors.'

* * *

Mike was talking about certain tablets he was taking and on which his life depended. 'They are vital for my continued existence,' he claimed, 'even if I didn't need them, I'd still have to take them.'

* * *

Pat went to the doctor and said, 'I've lost my voice, doctor.'
'I can hear that,' replied the doctor.

* * *

Pat was very ill indeed so Bridget sent for the doctor. After a brief examination the doctor announced that Pat was dead.
'I'm not,' cried Pat feebly from his bed.
'Be quiet,' said Bridget, 'do you know better than the doctor?'

* * *

Mike went to the doctor and told him he was suffering from hallucinations.
'Nonsense man,' said the doctor, 'you're just imagining things.'

* * *

Bridget: 'My father is a sexagenarian.'
Neighbour: 'For a man of his age, I think that's disgusting.'

* * *

Bridget was in a shoe shop and had tried on over a hundred pairs of shoes.

'I'm sorry,' she apologised to the assistant, 'the trouble is that one of my feet is bigger than the other.'

'Not at all madam,' said the placatory assistant, 'it's smaller if anything.'

* * *

Old Irish Proverb:
Death is the poor man's doctor.

* * *

Mike was badly injured in a shooting accident and the doctor reported on his four wounds as follows: — The first two wounds are fatal all right but the third and fourth are not and with good care and attention the patient should recover soon.

* * *

Pat was a masochist. There was nothing he liked better than a cold bath every morning so he always took a scalding hot bath instead.

* * *

Mike on the other hand was a sadist.

'Be nasty to me,' Pat used to implore him.

'No I won't,' Mike used to reply, 'I'll be nice to you.'

* * *

Bridget once passed a blind man sitting at a street corner, so, feeling sorry for him she threw tenpence into his box.

'That's a bit mean,' said the blind man at once, 'tenpence from a lady of means like yourself.'

'If you're blind,' retorted Bridget, 'how did you know it was tenpence I put in?'

'Actually,' said the man, 'I'm only sitting in for the regular blind man because it's his afternoon off — he's gone to the movies.'

* * *

Pat was attending a psychiatrist for a nervous complaint but when he found out that the fee was £50 per visit he told the shrink that he didn't want any more treatment.

Psychiatrist: 'If you think you're leaving here cured after only one visit, you're crazy.'

SOME DEATH CERTIFICATES

The patient didn't die of anything serious.

*   *   *

This man had never been fatally ill before.

*   *   *

Cause of death is unknown as the patient died without the aid of a doctor.

*   *   *

Went to bed feeling on top of the world but when he woke up he was dead.

*   *   *

The patient died of a Tuesday.

*   *   *

The cause of death was an act of God under very suspicious circumstances.

*   *   *

The patient died in a state of perfect health.

*   *   *

Suspected suicide, though the patient later denied this.

*   *   *

Under the section headed 'Cause of Death' on the death certificate one doctor signed his own name.

*   *   *

6

INDEFENCEBULL – JURIES AND THE LAW

What is it about jury service, courtrooms or any brush with the law that brings out the very worst in us and makes the sanest of people become gibbering idiots? According to some, the law is an ass rather than a bull, but this is a very fine distinction. Irish courtrooms and evidence given by Irish men and women throughout recorded history have been full of the most delicious bulls, blunders, lies and inconsistencies imaginable. Read any book of Irish legal memoirs (for example Maurice Healy's *The Old Munster Circuit)* and you will find dozens of examples of hilarious legal cases and cunning lawyers whose exploits were so imaginative that no fiction writer could have dreamed them up.

Irish wills too are a law unto themselves. The standard was set by that honorary Irishman Rabelais (surely a corruption of 'Robbie Lee') whose terse will is reputed to have run as follows:

I owe much and I have nothing – the rest I leave to the poor.

* * *

Mike was involved in a law case and was unfortunate enough to hire a solicitor notorious for his charges. On his final bill there were the following items:

Item: To crossing the street to discuss your case with you – 5 guineas.

Item: To re-crossing the street after discovering it wasn't you – 5 guineas.

* * *

Pat was being tried by jury, charged with stealing a horse. After a few hours of listening to boring evidence however he suddenly pleaded guilty. The judge instructed the jury to find him guilty, but to his amazement they retired for over an hour and returned a unanimous verdict of 'not guilty'. The judge protested that the defendant had pleaded guilty, but the foreman of the jury explained – 'you don't know him like we do, your honour. He's the biggest liar in the entire country and you can't believe a word out of his mouth.'

*　*　*

Mike once attended a very noisy trial where the judge suspended the trial for an hour, saying:
'It's so noisy in here that even when there's perfect silence you can't hear a single thing.'

*　*　*

Bridget was once charged with shoplifting but got off by pleading an alibi — she proved she was somewhere else when she committed the crime.

*　*　*

Pat was once convicted of a serious crime and just after sentence had been passed he confessed that he had actually been in jail when the crime was committed.
'Why on earth didn't you tell the court that?' his lawyer asked.
'I thought it might prejudice the jury against me,' said Pat.

*　*　*

Mike was fined £10 for being drunk but confessed to the judge that he had no money to pay the fine.
'You would have the money if you hadn't spent it on drink,' retorted the judge.

*　*　*

Pat was being defended by a lawyer who addressed the jury in the following immortal words:
'And, gentlemen, if I am wrong in this point, I have another point equally conclusive.'

*　*　*

Mike's lawyer, on the other hand, addressed the court as follows: 'We have to look back for centuries to find a parallel to this case, and even then we don't find it.'

*　*　*

Bridget was charged with reckless driving and causing the death of no less than twenty-four pigs. The prosecuting counsel was rubbing in the charges and emphasising the magnitude of the crime.

'Twenty-four pigs,' he thundered, 'twice the number in the jury box.'

* * *

Pat was called for service as a juryman in a major murder trial. However, he was challenged and asked, 'Do you believe in capital punishment?'

'Yes,' said Pat, 'if it's not too severe.'

* * *

One of the oldest bulls on record concerns a farmer who heard a lot of noise coming from his chicken coop one night and suspected burglars. So he went downstairs with his gun and shouted out 'is there anyone in there?'

Back came a squeaky voice, 'there's no one in here except us chickens.'

'That's all right,' said the farmer, 'but I could have sworn I heard a noise.'

* * *

Pat was charged with poaching a pair of rabbits. In defence he stated that the field from which he took them was 'alive with dead rabbits.'

* * *

'Are you innocent or guilty?' Bridget was asked in a court case.

'How can I tell,' asked Bridget, 'until I have heard the evidence?'

* * *

Mike was charged with perjury and, while not denying the charge, he stated in defence that he had too much respect for the truth than to be dragging it out on every occasion.

* * *

'When I sit on the bench,' an Irish judge is once said to have remarked, 'I promise to be neither partial nor impartial.'

* * *

Mike was charged with attempted murder because he threatened a woman with a knife.
'I didn't really intend to murder her your honour,' he told the judge, 'I just meant to frighten her to death.'

* * *

'You are charged,' said the Judge to Pat, 'with having wilfully, feloniously and with malice aforethought appropriated to your own use and behoof a certain article, to wit, a bovine quadruped — the aforementioned quadruped having been wrongfully and feloniously abstracted by you from the estate of one Daniel Murphy on or about the fourth day of July Anno Domini 1987 contrary to the law of the land. How do you plead?'
'Not guilty, your honour,' said Pat, 'sure all I did was steal a cow.'

* * *

'You leave this court,' said the judge to Mike, 'with no other stain on your character other than the fact that you were acquitted by a Limerick jury.'

* * *

Court crier: 'All you blackguards that aren't lawyers have to leave the court.'

* * *

SOME IRISH JURY VERDICTS

We find the man who stole the mare, not guilty.

*   *   *

We are unanimous − nine to three.

*   *   *

We find the defendant not guilty but recommend he does not do it again.

*   *   *

We recommend that the defendant be hanged and we hope it will be a lesson to him.

*   *   *

We find this man not guilty if he promises to give the money back.

*   *   *

We are of one mind − insane.

*   *   *

We find this woman not guilty if she will promise to emigrate.

*   *   *

We find the defendant guilty of innocently committing perjury.

*   *   *

We return a verdict of guilty against the unknown murderer who fired the alleged shot which killed O'Hara.

*   *   *

Our unanimous decision is that we want another barrel of Guinness.

*   *   *

We the jury have good friends on both sides of this case and would prefer not to get involved.

* * *

Mike once hired a verbiose lawyer who made very little sense but sounded very impressive. He addressed the jury as follows: 'this case is similar to the many cases of its kind that have been tried over the last hundred years.'

* * *

Bridget once did jury service in a murder trial and the defending lawyer addressed the jury thus: 'Ladies and gentlemen of the jury, think of the accused's mother, his only mother.'

* * *

In another case, Mike accused the police of brutality claiming that he had been handcuffed by the feet.

* * *

Under an old Irish law a witness cannot give evidence of his age unless he can remember being born. Otherwise, his testimony is treated as hearsay.

* * *

Here is a real-life Irish-American bull. Having jumped bail while awaiting a court appearance on a charge of car theft, the suspect surrendered to police after he saw a notice offering a $150 reward for information leading to his arrest. However, the reward committee unanimously turned down his request for the reward money.

* * *

When the judge called Mike an idiot he agreed. After all he was no fool.

Pat and Mike were escaping from jail and were being followed by the police with tracker dogs. They decided to climb into two trees to evade capture. As the dogs came sniffing to the base of Pat's tree, he went 'miaow, miaow.'

'Come away from that tree,' said the policeman to the dog, 'that's only a cat up there.'

Then the dog began to sniff at the base of Mike's tree.

'Moo, Moo,' went Mike.

*   *   *

Pat was up in court charged with bankruptcy. The judge asked him if he could pay anything at all towards the settlement that had been awarded against him.

'Not a penny, your honour,' said Pat, 'everything I own I've given to my lawyer and three of the jury.'

*   *   *

Mike was charged with stealing a goat but the judge told him that he was acquitted.

'Acquitted,' said Mike 'what does that mean? Does it mean I can keep the goat?'

*   *   *

Heard in an Irish court: 'Silence in court! Fifteen men have been convicted already without the judge being able to hear a single word of evidence because of the noise.'

*   *   *

Pat was charged with stealing horses and the judge told him that he could be tried by the judge himself or by a jury of his peers.

'What do you mean by "peers"?' asked Pat.

'Men and women,' said the judge, 'of your own class and equal.'

'Try me yourself judge,' said Pat, 'I don't want to be tried by a bunch of horse thieves.'

*   *   *

SOME IRISH WILLS

I leave everything to myself.

* * *

I leave everything to the doctor who pulls me through my final illness.

* * *

I leave my entire fortune for medical research in the hope that after I am dead a cure will be found for the disease from which I have died so that I can be cured and live to spend the money.

* * *

. . . . And finally to my no-good brother-in-law Sean whom I promised to mention in my will – hello there Sean.

* * *

An Irish farmer was settling his affairs with his solicitor. 'To each of my five sons I leave £50,000 and to each of my seven daughters I leave £30,000,' he said to the furiously typing solicitor.
'Hold on a moment,' said the solicitor, 'that comes to nearly half a million pounds, and you have assets of only £500, where is all this money to come from?'
'Blast them,' said the farmer, 'let them work for it like I did.'

* * *

Old Irish proverb –
Where there's a will, there are relatives.

* * *

7

BULLARNEY – THE JARVEY AND THE GILLIE

The wit and silver tongue of the jarvey are part of Irish folklore. These fellows live off their wits, delighting tourists with their blarney, flattery spread so thick that you can see right through it. The jarvey is the direct descendant of the gillie, the man who helped out on fishing trips or with hunting parties.

There are many stories about a jarvey called Dinny, now long since dead, who lived somewhere between Belfast and Killarney and who must have been the original stage Irishman.

*   *   *

Dinny was once faced with a huge crowd of tourists waiting to avail of his services. He remarked, 'If they all get on this jaunting car, there will be half of them left behind.'

*   *   *

Dinny was hurrying home on a dark night when his horse tripped in the pitch blackness and threw him on the road. He shook his fist at the sky and shouted out, 'blast you for a moon, you'd be out on a bright night.'

*   *   *

An elderly American tourist once asked Dinny what age he thought she was. He replied diplomatically, 'Begor madam, whatever age you are, you don't look it.'

*   *   *

Dinny was once driving a pair of elderly identical twins when they asked him which of them looked the younger. He replied diplomatically, 'each one of you looks younger than the other.'

*   *   *

Dinny was given a tip of tenpence after a long journey. He looked at it with contempt and said to his passenger, 'I feel I'm overpaid for this job.'

* * *

Passing by the local church tower a tourist noticed that each of the three clocks showed a different time so he asked Dinny for a reason. 'If they all showed the same time,' said Dinny with perfect logic, 'then there would be need for only one clock.'

* * *

Dinny once did a stint in Dublin driving tourists around and driving some of them mad.
'What's that building?' a passenger asked him one day.
'That's the Custom House,' he replied, 'and it's the strangest building in Ireland because the front is at the back'.

* * *

A tourist once asked Dinny if he spoke any other languages. 'How about Gaelic?' he questioned him, 'can you understand Gaelic?'
'Yes,' twinkled Dinny, 'if it's spoken in English.'
'How about Esperanto,' continued the tourist.
'I speak that like a native,' retorted Dinny.

* * *

Dinny had been reading books on Geography to impress his customers.
'Say, Dinny, where did all those rocks come from?' a passenger asked him one day.
'Those rocks,' said Dinny, proud of his knowledge, 'were laid down by massive glaciers as they came down from the mountains.'
'That's pretty good,' said the tourist. 'Tell me, where are all those glaciers now?'
Dinny was perplexed, but only for a moment.
'Gone back for more rocks,' he smiled.

* * *

Dinny drove his passengers to the edge of a cliff – the highest unprotected cliff in the South of Ireland.

'Say, this looks dangerous,' said an alarmed passenger, 'How come they don't have a warning notice here?'

'They did have,' said Dinny, 'but nobody ever fell over, so they took it away.'

* * *

'That,' said Dinny pointing to Carrantouhill, 'is Ireland's highest mountain.'

'Hold on,' said one of his passengers, 'that mountain beside it seems to be somewhat higher.'

'Begob you could be right,' said Dinny peering with his hand over his eyes. 'The trouble with Carrantouhill is that it's down in a hollow.'

* * *

Dinny was acting as boatman and the fishermen noticed that he would never either simply agree or disagree with them but qualified everything.

'That's a nice wind for sailing,' one of them remarked.

'It is,' said Dinny, 'but what there is of it is rather strong.'

* * *

Dinny lived in a little cottage way up in the mountains and one morning the postman arrived with a single letter for him.

'That's a long journey you had with a single letter,' said Dinny, 'you should have posted it.'

* * *

Dinny had two standard explanations to amuse his fishing clients. Firstly he claimed that pollution in the water was caused by all those dead fish swimming around, and secondly that the sea was salty because of all those herrings swimming around.

* * *

'What's the average tip you receive?' an English tourist, anxious to do the right thing, asked Dinny.

'Ten pounds,' said Dinny.

The tourist handed over ten pounds, feeling however that it was a bit much.

'Thank you, sir,' said Dinny having tucked the money safely away in his pocket, 'you're the first customer I've ever had that comes up to the average.'

* * *

Dinny had taken a party of fishermen around a lake and they had a very successful day's fishing, so they invited him into their posh hotel for a drink. In the lounge were a dozen heads of deer proudly mounted on the wall.

'What do you think of those?' Dinny was asked.

'Well,' said Dinny thoughtfully, 'that herd of deer must have been travelling at a fair old pace when they hit that wall.'

* * *

'Are there many fish in this river?" a tourist asked Dinny.

'It's so bad,' said Dinny 'that people can't take water out of it because of the taste of salmon on their tea.'

* * *

The horse under Dinny's jaunting car looked a bit thin so a tourist suggested that he might fatten up the horse a bit.

'Certainly not,' said Dinny, 'the poor baste is so thin he is hardly fit to carry the little flesh he has on him already.'

* * *

Any time he saw a rainbow, Dinny used to remark to his passengers, 'The rainbow is not an optical illusion – it only looks like one.'

* * *

'Do you believe in ghosts?' a passenger once asked Dinny.
'Indeed I do not,' he replied, 'I've seen too many of them to believe in them.'

* * *

'Most of the things you tell us,' one of his passengers remarked to Dinny, 'are either improbable or impossible.'
'Ireland,' said Dinny, 'is a country where the improbable frequently happens and the impossible always happens.'

* * *

'Who lives in that fine house we're passing?' Dinny was asked.
'A man from London, who never sets foot in this place,' said Dinny, 'the whole country is crawling with absentee landlords.'

* * *

Dinny's fishing party were on the lake but weren't having any luck.
'Look here,' complained one of them bitterly, 'we've been on this lake for over six hours and haven't had a single bite.'
'We're not nearly as bad as last week's party,' said Dinny cheerfully, 'they were twelve hours in the boat without a single bite.'

* * *

An Englishman came over to Ireland for a week's fishing and hired Dinny as his gillie. In the entire week, however, he caught only one salmon.
'Do you know,' he said to Dinny as he departed, 'this salmon cost me £500?'
'Weren't you lucky,' smiled Dinny, 'that you didn't catch two of them.'

* * *

Dinny once took an Oriental Indian prince on a fishing trip and the prince was lucky enough to feel a nibble on his line. Dinny's exhortations went as follows:

'Hold him, your highness, play him, your honour; give him more line, your worship; pull him in, your lordship; ah you've lost him, you foreign bastard.'

* * *

One of Dinny's clients hooked a very small fish only a few inches long and after a fierce battle managed to bring it to the end of his rod.
'What do I do now?' asked the helpless fisherman.
'Maybe,' smiled Dinny, 'you could take a knife, climb up the rod and stab it to death.'

* * *

Dinny was in the habit of throwing back any fish over a foot long because his frying pan was only twelve inches wide.

* * *

'Have you ever read *The Penguin Book of Quotations?*' a literary client asked Dinny.
'No sir,' said Dinny, 'I didn't even know that penguins could talk.'

* * *

'Do you believe in fairies?' Dinny was asked.
'I don't,' said Dinny, 'but I know they are there and that they probably don't believe in me either.'

* * *

'How well do you know this lake?' a client asked Dinny while they were in a boat together.
'I know every rock in this lake,' said Dinny. There followed a mighty crash. 'That,' said Dinny, 'was one of the biggest rocks just now.'

* * *

Dinny on a very rainy day visited an art gallery but refused to pay because he was only looking.

* * *

Dinny always brought his boat as close in to the pier·as possible and never left a gap. This was because in his youth he jumped across the gap but fell in the middle before he got half way.

* * *

Said Dinny to a client who claimed to have caught a fish so heavy that its photograph alone weighed twenty pounds, 'I've told you a million times not to exaggerate.'

* * *

Dinny once boasted that he personally caught a fish so big that when he hauled him ashore the level of the lake fell by ten feet.

* * *

Dinny once came across a postcard left behind in his jaunting car.
It read: Having a lovely time in Ireland; wish you were here. In the space for the address, under the stamp was written — 'have forgotten your address.'

* * *

Dinny had a notice beside his boat.
BOAT FOR HIRE — FISHING OR PLEASURE.

* * *

8

SIR BULL ROACH – FATHER OF THE HERD

Sir Boyle Roach is generally acknowledged to be the father of the Irish bull. Born in 1743 he was a member of the Irish Parliament for the district of Tralee in 1775. So many bulls have been attributed to him that he couldn't possibly have had time to utter them all. In fact if he were alive to-day he would probably turn in his grave to hear all the bulls that are uttered in his name. Actually the best known one associated with his name – 'why should we do anything for posterity, what has posterity ever done for us?' – had been calved by Addison some thirty years before his birth. However, he is on record as saying that if the revolution ever came to Ireland, the rebels would 'cut people to mince meat and throw their bleeding heads on the table to stare them in the face.'

Some of his alleged bulls however were more apparent than real. When he referred to 'a certain anonymous author called Junius', he was merely referring to the fact that Junius was the pen name used by an anonymous Roman author. There are those who claim that Boyle Roach's speeches were written for him by others and that he delivered his speeches without notes and so recalled the words rather than the sense. Others claim that he was a wily old gentleman whose bulls were quite deliberate and made in order to draw attention to himself. Whatever the truth of the matter, many fine bulls were sired by him and in this chapter we present a few of them, together with his famous letter.

*   *   *

Boyle Roach's bird was legendary. 'No man,' he declared 'can be in two places at the one time, unless he is a bird.'

*   *   *

The man who would stoop so low as to write an anonymous letter, the least he might do is to sign his name to it.

* * *

Mr. Speaker, the country is in such a desperate state that little children, who can neither walk nor talk, are running around the street cursing their maker.

* * *

I answer in the affirmative with an emphatic 'NO!'

* * *

I would give up half − nay, the whole of the constitution to preserve the remainder.

* * *

Sir Boyle once proposed that all wooden gates in Ireland should be made of iron.

* * *

On another occasion, Sir Boyle Roach declared that the tax on leather would be severely felt by the barefooted peasantry of Ireland. 'But,' he continued, 'this situation could easily be remedied by making the under-leathers of wood.'

* * *

In 1784 the Parliament of which Sir Boyle was a member introduced a bill containing the following clause:
'If a member is unable to write, he may authorise another person to frank for him, provided that on the back of the letter so franked the member gives a certificate under his hand of his inability to write.'

* * *

The people of this country are living from hand to mouth like the birds of the air.

* * *

Sir Boyle said of the Act of Union that it would change the barren hills into fruitful valleys.

* * *

When other members laughed at Boyle Roach's bull 'why should we do anything for posterity, what has posterity ever done for us', he is said to have continued, 'By posterity, gentlemen, I do not mean our ancestors, but those who came immediately after them.'

* * *

Boyle Roach once proposed that every quart bottle should hold a quart.

* * *

Single misfortunes rarely come alone and the worst of all misfortunes is usually followed by a greater misfortune.

* * *

The only way of preventing what is past is to put to a stop to it before it happens.

* * *

Boyle Roach accused an opposition member of being the sort of man who would pat you on the back in front of your face but who would stab you in the chest once your back was turned.

* * *

To stop smuggling on the Shannon, two frigates should be stationed on opposite points at the mouth of the river and there they should remain with strict orders not to stir; and so by cruising up and down they would be able to stop everything that passed between them.

* * *

The cup of Ireland's miseries has been overflowing for centuries, but it is not yet full.

* * *

Many hundreds of people were destitute even of the very goods they possess.

* * *

Iron gates will last forever and afterwards they can be used for making horse shoes.

* * *

It was said of Sir Boyle Roach that he never opened his mouth without putting his foot in it.

* * *

In opposing certain reforms in the legal system Boyle Roach said, 'By trial by jury I have lived, and please God with trial by jury I shall die.'

* * *

In favour of the Act of Union: 'Gentlemen may titter and titter and may think it a bad measure: but when the day of judgement comes, then honourable gentlemen will be satisfied with this most excellent union.'

* * *

Three-quarters of what the opposition say about us is lies and the other half is without any foundation in truth.

* * *

It used to be said that whenever Boyle Roach opened his mouth, a bull flew out.

* * *

The only living beasts on the farms of Ireland are the birds that fly over them.

*   *   *

Letter written by Sir Boyle Roche during the Irish Rebellion:
Dear Sir,

Having now a little peace and quiet, I sit down to inform you of the bustle and confusion we are in from the bloodthirsty rebels, many of whom are now, thank God, killed and dispersed. To give you some idea of the danger we are in, I will only say that while I am writing this letter I have a sword in one hand and a pistol in the other. We are in a pretty mess; can get nothing to eat, and no wine to drink except whiskey. When we sit down to dinner we are obliged to keep both hands armed. I conclude from the beginning that this would be the end; and I am right, for it is not half over yet. At present there are such goings on that everything is at a standstill. I should have answered your letter a fortnight ago, but I only received it this morning; indeed, hardly a mail arrives safe without being robbed. No longer ago than yesterday the mail coach from Dublin was robbed near this town; the bags had been judiciously left behind for fear of accident, and by great good luck there was nobody in the coach except two outside passengers, who had nothing for the thieves to take. Last Thursday an alarm was given that a gang of rebels, in full retreat from Drogheda, were advancing under the French standard; but they had no colors, nor any drums except bagpipes. Immediately every man in the place, including women and children, ran out to meet them. We soon found our forces a great deal too little, and were far too near to think of retreating. Death was in every face, and to it we went. By the time half our party were killed we began to be all alive. Fortunately the rebels had no guns, except pistols, cutlasses, and pikes; and we had plenty of muskets and ammunition. We put them all to the sword; not a soul of them escaped alive except some that were drowned in the adjoining bog. In fact, in a short time nothing was heard but silence. Their uniforms were all different — chiefly green. After the action was over we went to rummage their camp. All we found was a few pikes without heads, a parcel of empty bottles filled with water, and a bundle of blank French commissions filled up with Irish names. Troops are now stationed round, which exactly squares with my ideas of security. Adieu. I have only time to add, that I am yours in haste, B.R.

P.S. — If you do not receive this, of course it must have miscarried; therefore I beg you write and let me know.

9

KITH AND KINE – THE FAMILY

The Irish family is a closely-knit one (some would say a close collection of nits) and family matters very much in human affairs.   Where there is some important human activity or institution, there will be jokes and the Irish family is no exception – children, parents, relations and in-laws all grab part of the action.   Pat and Bridget are of course man and wife and Mike is almost part of the family.

* * *

When Pat and Bridget's first baby was born, the first question Mike asked was 'is it a boy or a child?'

* * *

Pat and Bridget had twin boys and she was asked how she could tell them apart. She replied, 'I stick my finger in Tim's mouth and if he bites me I know it's Frank. Anyway, Tim is an identical twin but Frank isn't.'
Asked if the twins cried at night, she replied, 'Each of them cries so loud you can't hear the other.'

* * *

Mike was asked if he had any photographs of himself as a baby. He said that he hadn't but that he was going to have one taken.

* * *

Old Irish Proverb –
It's a good thing for your wife that you're not married.

* * *

Pat was philosophising about the terrible state of the world. 'The happiest man,' he declared, 'is the man who has never been born. But such is the nature of life that this is a privilege granted only to one in a million.'

* * *

After Pat died, Bridget decided that she would like to have a nice photograph to remember him by, but the only one she could find had him wearing a loud and vulgar cap. She took the photograph to a professional photographer and asked him if he could remove the cap and touch up the photograph. 'Certainly,' he replied, 'I'll do that. Tell me, which side did he part his hair on?'

'Won't you see that when you take his cap off?' said Bridget.

* * *

Mike was seen wearing a new suit one morning and a friend asked why. 'Well,' he replied, 'I'm loading a cart of manure this morning and I'm getting married this afternoon. I'll save time because I'll only have to change my vest and underwear.'

* * *

When the family squabbles got too much for her, Bridget used to say to Pat, 'Happy are the parents who have no children.'

* * *

'Insanity is hereditary,' said Mike, 'you can get it from your children.'

* * *

After Pat was away from home for three years, his wife Bridget had a baby. Mike asked him if he was a bit suspicious about the happy event.

'Certainly not,' beamed Pat, 'there was five years between me and my brother.'

* * *

Bridget applied for a divorce from Pat on the grounds that her last two children were not his.

* * *

Mike told a friend that he hadn't got a living relative in the world except for a cousin who died in America three years ago.

*　*　*

Pat claimed that his family was one of the oldest in Ireland. He had a book on the history of the family and in chapter four there was a footnote which read, 'About this time the world was created.' Most of the family records were lost in the Flood. Mike tried to top this by saying that his ancestors had been with Noah in the Ark.
'That's nothing,' said Pat, 'at the time of the Flood, our family had their own boat.'

*　*　*

Bridget wrote to all her relatives in November, explaining that because of the postal expense she wouldn't be sending them any Christmas greetings this year.

*　*　*

Every year Pat threw a huge family party that went on and on and on. In fact nobody ever went home until everyone else was gone.

*　*　*

Looking at all his nephews and nieces, Mike declared that youth is too wonderful a thing to be wasted on young people.

*　*　*

Pat complained that Bridget was a poor housekeeper and spent very little time in the house. 'In fact,' he declared, 'for every time she comes in, she goes out three times.'

*　*　*

Pat and Bridget hired a babysitter for their little boy but she couldn't keep him quiet unless she let him make a noise. She complained that baby was good only when he was being naughty.

*　*　*

Mike was very ugly, but he claimed that he had been born a very beautiful baby and a jealous nurse had exchanged him at birth.

* * *

'Is Bill a relative of yours?' Pat asked Mike.
'He's a distant relative,' said Mike, 'I was my parents' first child and he was their twelfth.'

* * *

Bridget was on her first visit to Dublin and saw a black man for the first time. Her comment was, 'Thank God I was born at home.'

* * *

Mike was missing for a few weeks so his family issued the following description to the police: 'Age not known, but looks older than he is.'

* * *

Mike: 'Was the latest child a boy or a girl, Pat?'
Pat: 'Have a guess, Mike.'
Mike: 'It was a girl.'
Pat: 'No, guess again.'
Mike: 'It was a boy.'
Pat: 'Ah, someone must have told you.'

* * *

When Mike's mother died, he was heard to lament 'She was the best mother I ever had.'

* * *

Pat was inclined to hide behind the newspaper in the evenings to protect himself from Bridget's idle chatter.
Bridget: 'You're paying as little attention to me as if I was a dumb baste in the fields talking to you.'

* * *

Mike complained to Pat that he never came to visit him. 'If I lived as near to you,' he told him, 'as you lived to me, I'd come to see you often.'

* * *

When Pat joined the army he forgot to take his big overcoat with him so Bridget posted it to him. To save weight, she cut off the metal buttons and put them in one of the pockets.

* * *

Mike had a very strict father. His favourite saying to his children was 'Silence when you speak to me.'

* * *

Bridget to Pat: 'If you shaved every day you wouldn't have to shave so often.'

* * *

'That's a beautiful child you have there,' said a neighbour to Bridget.
'That's nothing,' said Bridget, 'you should see his photograph.'

* * *

Mike was up in court charged, among other things, with giving a wrong name to the policeman.
'Why did you tell the policeman your name was Tom O'Sullivan, when it was Des MacHale?' asked the judge.
'Your honour,' Mick replied, 'my mother was married twice.'

* * *

Bridget never put milk in the fridge as soon as it was delivered — she always gave the fridge some time to warm up first.

* * *

Pat described a woman he met as 'the ugliest woman in the world.' Her sister called round and threatened to sue him if he did not issue an immediate apology. Pat's statement read: — 'Yesterday I described Miss X as the ugliest woman in the world. Now that I have seen her sister, I wish to withdraw that statement.'

* * *

Mike was giving Pat the run of his new flat. 'Here's a key,' he told him, 'but the lock doesn't work. Neither does the bell, but if you want to get in just give the door a good kick.'

* * *

'Who was that at the door?' Bridget asked Pat one evening after there was a knock at the door.
'Nobody,' said Pat, 'just a man looking for the wrong house.'

* * *

When Mike went to America he visited P.T. Barnum's famous exhibition of circus freaks. He was particularly fascinated by the famous Siamese twins.
'Is it true that they are brothers?' he asked Barnum.
'Yes it is,' said Barnum.
'Wasn't it the mercy of providence,' said Mike, 'to make them brothers and not to have two total strangers tied together for life.'

* * *

Pat was sitting in the bar at Shannon Airport when he got into conversation with an American.
'I've come to meet my brother,' said Pat, 'it's his first trip home from America in forty years.'
'Will you be able to recognise him?' asked the American.
'I'm sure I won't,' said Pat, 'after all those years.'
'I wonder if he will recognise you?' said the American.
'Of course he will,' said Pat, 'sure I haven't been away at all.'

* * *

Bridget was warning her little girl about the dangers of being molested. 'Be careful coming and going to school,' she warned her, 'and don't speak to any strangers unless you know them.'

* * *

'What is Tom's other name?' Pat asked Mike.
'Tom who?' asked Mike.

* * *

Bridget was applying for a passport.
'Are you a natural born Irish subject?' she was asked.
'No,' she replied, 'I was a Caesarian birth.'

* * *

To save money, Bridget used to buy the Pill in twin packs.

* * *

10

BULLIGERENCE, BULLFIGHTING, ACT OF SERVICE BULLETS AND SPORTING BULLS

'The Irish,' said Samuel Johnson, 'are a fair people — they never speak well of each other.' Someone else added, 'The Irish are at peace only when they are fighting.' This reputation, it must be admitted, is probably deserved, and it has been well said that the Irish don't know what they want, but will fight like hell until they get it. That old bulldog himself, Winston Churchill, said that whenever England thought she had got the answer to the Irish question, the Irish changed the question.

In this chapter we look at the bulls involved in war and fighting and in the army, and because Irish sports fields sometimes resemble battlefields, we have included sporting bulls as well.

*   *   *

Pat was sleeping one night when he thought he heard a burglar in the room, so he took the shotgun that he always kept by his bedside and left fly a few rounds, narrowly missing his own toes. On getting up and finding that it was a false alarm, he exclaimed, 'thank God I didn't have the bed turned the other way round or I would have blown my head off.'

*   *   *

'Do you need a police station in your village?' Mike was asked in a survey.
'No,' said Mike, 'although we have one. But if we didn't have one, we would need one.'

*   *   *

Bridget saw a film in which there was a man lying dead with a bullet hole in the middle of his forehead.

'Wasn't it the mercy of God,' she declared, 'that it didn't go through the unfortunate man's eye.'

* * *

Pat bought a racing greyhound but found that the cost of feeding it was prohibitive. So every day he halved the amount of food he had given the day previously and for a time the dog seemed to manage quite well. Then, however, the dog died. 'Blast it,' said Pat, 'just as I was managing to feed him on nothing at all, he went and died on me.'

* * *

Mike once boasted that he had got in free into the All-Ireland football final by bribing one of the men on the gate with £20.

* * *

Pat joined the air force and was asked to test a new type of parachute. No, it wasn't the type that opened on impact, it was the type that opened when ten feet from the ground. The theory was that if it failed to open at that height, then the jumper wouldn't have very far to fall. On Pat's first jump from 10,000 feet he didn't wear a parachute at all, because it was only a practice jump.

* * *

Mike's wife wasn't happy about him joining the army.

'If you lose both your legs in the battle,' she warned him, 'don't come running home to me.'

* * *

Pat and Mike were out hunting rabbits when they saw a fine specimen.

'Quick Mike,' said Pat, 'shoot him.'

'I can't,' said Mike, 'I've run out of ammunition.'

'Look,' said Pat, 'I know that, you know that, but the rabbit doesn't know that.'

* * *

Bridget once entered a competition to predict the score in the All-Ireland football final. First prize was two tickets for the match.

* * *

Pat and Mike were lying in wait one night for their sworn enemy in order to beat him to a pulp. After about three hours Pat said to Mike, 'he's late, I hope to God nothing has happened to the poor fellow.'

* * *

In the heat of battle Mike shouted to his men – 'keep firing men and don't let the enemy know you are out of ammunition.'

* * *

Pat in his youth was a noted football referee. He developed a new technique of having extra time before the match began in case of fog.

* * *

Mike joined the army but came a cropper while out drilling on the parade ground. He tripped over a hole that was sticking right up out of the ground.

* * *

Pat and Mike were having a fight and the insults began to fly. 'Say another thing like that to me,' said Pat, 'and I'll knock the brains out of your empty head.'

* * *

Bridget took up middle distance running but wasn't very successful in competitions. Then after many attempts she finally won a race.
'I'm first at last,' she declared, 'I was always behind before.'

* * *

Pat and Mike joined the army and were being drilled by a sergeant.

'Fall out and just look at yourselves,' he shouted, 'If I could see which of you two fools is out of step, I would put him in the guard house.'

* * *

The sergeant told Mike to go and stand at the end of the line. Mike came back and told him there was someone standing there already.

* * *

Pat joined the 75th Regiment of the Army to be near his brother who was in the 76th Regiment.

* * *

'This is a crooked card game,' remarked Mike one evening, 'someone isn't playing the hand I dealt him.'

* * *

Bridget was in a philosophical mood one evening. 'Thank God for water,' she remarked, 'because if there was no water, no one could learn how to swim and we would all drown.'

* * *

Pat and Mike were fighting a duel and each was trying to gain some advantage over the other.

Said Pat: 'can I stand ten paces nearer to you than you stand to me because I've lost the sight of one eye entirely?'

'No,' said Mike, 'but because you're much fatter than I am, I will draw a chalk outline my size on your body, and any shots outside that line will not count.'

* * *

'What's all that noise?' Bridget asked Pat one evening.

'It's nothing dear,' said Pat, 'they're just forcing some men to join the Volunteers.'

* * *

Mike was telling his children how ungrateful they were. 'I died,' he told them, 'in the Civil War, to make this country free for people like you.'

* * *

'What struck me most about the war,' said Pat, 'was the number of bullets that missed me.'

* * *

'Why did you hit Mike?' the judge asked Pat.
'Well your honour,' said Pat, 'I knew he was going to hit me so I retaliated first.'

* * *

'Have you ever shot a bird Mike?' Bridget asked.
'The only bird I ever shot,' said Mike, 'was a squirrel, which I killed with a stone which caused it to drop out of a tree and into a river in which it drowned.'

* * *

Pat said that his most abiding memory of the army was the announcement, 'Please inform the troops that communications have completely broken down.'

* * *

'What are you two fighting about?' a policeman asked Pat and Mike one night.
'We're not fighting,' they told him, 'we're just trying to separate ourselves from each other.'

* * *

Bridget fell in the kitchen one evening and Pat said to her, 'Are you hurt, my love? Come over here and let me pick you up.'

* * *

Stephen Leacock's description of a horseman must surely be classed as an Irish bull:
'He jumped on his horse and galloped off madly in all directions.'

* * *

Pat and Mike were out hunting duck when Pat took a fine shot, hit a duck and it fell at their feet.
Turning to Mike, he expected a glowing compliment.
'You could have saved your shot,' said Mike casually, 'the fall would have killed it anyway.'

* * *

Pat was wearing a top hat when somebody fired a shot at him and it went right through the top of the hat. Bridget declared 'weren't you lucky you weren't wearing a low hat.'

* * *

'My brother Tom,' boasted Mike, 'was the finest fighter in the country. Although he had only one arm, he used to dispose of opponents two at a time by banging their heads together.'
'I thought you said he had only one arm,' objected Pat.
'When my brother got into a fight,' said Mike, 'he forgot all about that.'

* * *

Bridget's new parrot escaped and flew to the top of the nearest tree. Bravely, Mike climbed the tree and was putting his hand out to catch it when the parrot said, 'What are you doing, what are you doing?'
'Oh, I'm sorry sir,' said Mike, pulling back, 'I thought you were a bird.'

* * *

Pat entered in the Cork City Marathon Race but Mike decided that he wasn't fit enough to compete. He merely ran round all the way behind Pat to encourage him.

* * *

Pat was fishing and it started to rain, so he went under a bridge for shelter.
'You're not afraid of a few drops of rain are you?' Mike taunted him.
'Not at all,' said Pat, 'the fish come in here to shelter too.'

* * *

Mike once boasted that he caught a fish so big that after he landed it, the level of the lake fell by ten feet.

* * *

Pat was drilling a local force of volunteer soldiers.
'All of you without arms,' he ordered them, 'raise your hands.'

* * *

Mike emigrated and decided on a military career. He joined the Swiss Horse Marines.

* * *

And finally, an English Bull from the Mother of Parliaments. The following bovine statement was made by an English Politician during the London bombings of the Seventies:

The trouble with hoax bomb calls nowadays is that you've got to take them so seriously. In the old days you knew they were hoax bomb calls.

* * *

11

BULLS AND BEARS – BUSINESS AND MONEY

There is a saying in Ireland – Money isn't everything; for a start it isn't even plentiful, and it must be admitted that the Irish have a pragmatic approach (whatever that means) to financial matters. They feel that money was made to be spent and that if you hold on to money for too long, it is inclined to burn a hole in your pocket. Maybe this attitude stems from the stories of fairy gold which turned to dust in your purse.

Financial dealings and the complexity of money systems give rise to a great deal of bulls and blunders especially when they confront the common man and woman and nobody could be commoner than Pat, Mike and Bridget.

* * *

Pat heard that there had been a run on the bank and that his money was all gone so he rushed to his local branch and demanded to withdraw it.
'Certainly,' said the manager, 'how would you like it?'
'Oh,' said Pat, 'If you've got it, I don't want it, but if you haven't got it, I do want it.'

* * *

Bridget was trying to cash a cheque in an out of town bank.
'Can you identify yourself, madam?' asked the clerk.
'Certainly,' said Bridget, reaching into her handbag. She took out a little mirror, looked in it and declared confidently, 'yes it's me all right, I'd recognise me anywhere.'

* * *

Mike was on his way home from the cattle fair having sold all his cows.
'Did you get what you expected for them?' Pat asked.
'No,' said Mike, 'but then I didn't expect I would.'

* * *

'Money doesn't buy happiness,' said Bridget, 'after all, a man with ten million pounds is no happier than a man with nine million pounds.'

* * *

Pat disclosed to Mike that he kept £20,000 under a mattress in his bedroom. Mike asked him why he didn't keep it in the bank in view of all the interest he would get.
'I've thought of that,' said Pat, 'I put a little away for the interest every week too.'

* * *

Bridget went into a grocer's shop and asked for some lemons. 'We have those now madam,' said the assistant, 'but we're out of them at the moment.'

* * *

Pat and Mike were a bit the worse for drink.
Pat: 'Haven't I seen you somewhere before?'
Mike: 'I don't think so.'
Pat: 'I'm sure I met you at a big financial conference in Dublin a few years ago.'
Mike: 'I've never been to Dublin.'
Pat: 'Neither have I. It must have been two other fellows.'

* * *

Bridget went to the grocer's shop to buy butter.
'How much does it cost?' she asked him.
'£2 a pound,' he replied.
'In the shop down the road,' she retorted, 'it only costs £1 a pound.'
'Why don't you buy it there then?' he asked her.
'They're out of stock,' said Bridget.
'Well when I'm out of stock,' he told her, I only charge 70 pence a pound.'
'All right then,' said Bridget, 'I'll come back when you're out of stock.'

* * *

'The Post Office,' declared Mike, 'is the only convenient place to keep your money. You can draw it out at any instant if you give two weeks notice.'

* * *

'I cannot understand,' said Bridget, 'how the milk company is complaining about a shortage of glass milk bottles. I've got thousands of them at home.'

* * *

'Every man,' said Pat, 'should live within his income, even if he has to borrow to do so.'

* * *

Mike went to the petrol station and asked the assistant for £10 worth of petrol. Rather ashamed of the size of his order, he remarked to the assistant, 'Before the price went up, I used to buy £20 worth.'

* * *

'Life insurance,' declared Pat, 'is a scheme whereby you must live poor so that you'll be rich when you die.'

* * *

'It's a funny thing,' said Bridget, 'that the poor, the people who need money the most, are always the very ones who never seem to have it.'

* * *

Mike arrived home from town and announced that he had just acquired a bottle of whiskey.
'How did you manage that?' his wife asked.
'Well,' said Mike, 'it was reduced from £10 to £5 so I bought it with the £5 I saved.'

* * *

Pat went into his bank and asked the manager for a loan. When the manager agreed to do so, Pat said 'Right that's it, I'm withdrawing all my money from this bank immediately. I can't trust an institution that is prepared to lend to such a poor risk as me.'

* * *

'A bank,' said Bridget, 'is an institution that will lend you money only when you can produce enough collateral to prove you don't need money in the first place.'

* * *

Mike was asked to give an estimate of how much a house he was building would cost. He included in his estimate an estimate of how much the estimate would be less than the correct figure.

* * *

'Is this seed guaranteed?' Bridget asked the storekeeper. 'Madam,' he replied, 'any seed that doesn't grow, bring it back and we will refund your money.'

* * *

Pat was drinking in a pub one night when the landlord asked him if he was going to pay for the drink he had just had. 'Did you pay for it?' asked Pat.
'Yes,' said the landlord, 'I have to pay cash for all my stock.'
'Well,' said Pat, 'there's no point in both of us paying for it, is there?'

* * *

Under the corrupt election system, Mike was offered £10 to vote for the first political party, £8 to vote for the second, and £5 to vote for the third. He voted for the third party because he figured they were the least corrupt.

* * *

Pat was returning home late one night when he was attacked by a mugger.

'Your money or your life,' shouted the mugger.

'You'd better take my life,' said Pat, 'I'm saving my money for my old age.'

*　　*　　*

At the time of the revolution in Ireland, it was suggested that all English money in the country should be collected and burned.

*　　*　　*

Bridget went into the baker's shop and asked, 'Is that bread today's, because yesterday's was not?'

*　　*　　*

Mike was offered a government grant to generate electricity by setting up a dozen windmills on his land.

He complained, 'There's hardly enough wind in this part of the country to keep a single windmill in operation, let alone a dozen of them.'

*　　*　　*

Bridget called round to her insurance office to make a claim for fire damage. The clerk asked her if she had a certified list of all the articles that had been lost in the fire. 'I did have,' said Bridget, 'but it was burned with the rest of my effects.'

*　　*　　*

Mike was making his will. 'I want my money divided equally between my sons and daughters,' he declared, 'and I leave the residue to my lawyer.'

*　　*　　*

'Dublin is a great city to live in,' declared Pat, 'but it's no place for a poor man unless he has lots of money.'

* * *

'What would you do if you found a million pounds, Mike?' Bridget asked.
'Well it all depends,' said Mike, 'who had lost it. If it was a poor person, I'd certainly return it.'

* * *

'How could anyone live on £50 a week,' demanded Pat, 'especially when he hasn't got it?'

* * *

Comment on a failed Irish businessman — that fellow has a great future behind him.

* * *

Mike was complaining that his landlord demanded one-tenth of his income as rent. 'And if he had his way,' he declared, 'he would demand as much as one-twentieth.'

* * *

Bridget received the following letter from her son in college.
Dear Mother,
    Send me £50 immediately.
    Your loving son,
    Ignatius.
P.S. I am so ashamed to have written this letter asking you for money that I sent a friend to retrieve it but the postman had already collected it. I can only hope that it was lost in the post.

Bridget replied.
Dear Son,
    Do not worry. The letter was lost in the post.
    Your loving mother,
    Bridget
P.S. I would have enclosed £50 but I have already sealed the envelope.

* * *

Pat's bank manager called him into his office to inform him that his current account was heavily overdrawn.
'I'm terribly sorry,' said Pat, 'can I give you a cheque?'

*　　*　　*

When decimal currency was introduced into Ireland for the first time, Bridget complained bitterly about the effect on people who had been used to the old system all their lives.
'Couldn't they have waited,' she asked, 'until all the old people had died?'

*　　*　　*

'Pat,' said Mike,'here's that pound I borrowed from you last week.'
'Sure Mike,' replied Pat, 'I had forgotten all about it.'
'Why the hell didn't you say that then,' retorted Mike.

*　　*　　*

Bridget went to an auction and noticed the following entry in the catalogue.
Lot 314 One pair unique Irish silver mugs.
Lot 315 Another pair.

*　　*　　*

'Good morning Pat, and how are you to-day,' said the post-mistress.
'Very well,' replied Pat, 'I've come to collect my pension.'
'Do you have any identification, Pat?' she asked.

*　　*　　*

Mike applied for a rates rebate from his local council and received the following reply:
Dear Sir,
　　　　Rate rebates are only for people with low incomes and as you have no income at all, you are not eligible.

*　　*　　*

12

BULLING AND COWING –
LOVABULL AND INCOMPATABULL
– COBULLATION

Ireland has the highest average age for marriage in the world – 31 for men and 26 for women. On the other hand families tend to be large and it is not uncommon to find fathers up to fifty years older than their children. Courtships in Ireland are long drawn-out affairs during which the girl decides if she can do any better. During these long courtships, the reluctant male communicates with his wife-to-be mostly verbally – hence the bulls and blunders.

In Ireland, marriage is an institution – but who wants to live in an institution. George Bernard Shaw said that it would always be a popular institution because it combined a maximum of temptation with a maximum of opportunity. Oscar Wilde, just the sort of man you could trust with your daughter, claimed that a man can be happy with any woman as long as he does not love her. He of course could resist everything except temptation. And let us not forget two relevant old Irish proverbs:

> Love is a temporary insanity curable by marriage and
> There are only three kinds of woman a man cannot understand – a young woman, a middle-aged woman and an old woman.

* * *

You should have seen the engagement ring that Pat bought for Bridget. It had two diamonds, three rubies and a sapphire – all missing.

* * *

'The only man,' said Mike, 'who knows how to manage his wife is a bachelor.'

* * *

Pat and Bridget had a stormy marriage. In fact the only thing they had in common was that they disagreed about everything.

*   *   *

When Pat and Bridget were out courting in Pat's car one night he began to feel a bit passionate.
'Get into the back seat,' he whispered.
'No, Pat, I won't,' replied Bridget.
'Why won't you get into the back seat, Bridget?' he asked.
'Because,' said Bridget, 'I'd prefer to stay here in the front seat with you.'

*   *   *

'The weaker sex,' declared Mike, 'is the stronger sex, because of the weakness of the stronger sex for the weaker sex.'

*   *   *

Pat and Bridget were visiting the zoo when an unmerciful fight broke out between them. Pat took to his heels and took refuge in the lion's cage.
'Come out of there, you coward,' shouted Bridget.

*   *   *

Pat and Bridget's daughter ran away with a married man who had lost both his legs.

*   *   *

Mike was delighted when his wife went on a severe diet. She was losing three pounds a week and he reckoned he would be rid of her in two years.

*   *   *

'I believe in chivalry,' declared Pat, 'I'll defend a woman against any man but myself.'

*   *   *

'It's a great pleasure,' Mike used to say, 'to be alone, especially when your sweetheart is with you.'

* * *

When Pat and Bridget were courting, Pat was very shy in popping the question and Bridget was equally slow in giving a definite answer. Finally, he wrote twice to her proposing marriage but received no reply. In desperation he wrote to her for the third time as follows:
Dear Bridget,
    This is the third time I've written to you proposing. If the answer is no, I hope you have the decency to return this letter unopened.

* * *

'You think you're a beauty,' said Mike to his girl friend one evening in exasperation, 'but I see a dozen more beautiful women than you on the street every day with my eyes shut.'

* * *

Bridget was so pestered by Pat's attentions when they first met that she married him just to get rid of him — and it worked beyond her wildest expectations.

* * *

Mike and his wife were going through a stormy patch so he even initiated divorce proceedings. However, he withdrew them quickly in case his wife got to hear of it.

* * *

'Women,' declared Pat, 'are mighty similar in one way — no two of them are alike.'

* * *

Pat and Bridget were having a row and although she admitted it was fundamentally her fault she said to him 'I'm sorry Pat, but I won't apologise.'

* * *

'Do you dream about me?' Bridget asked Pat.
'Sure,' said Pat, 'I can't sleep with dreaming of you love.'

* * *

'How are you getting on with your new wife?' Mike was asked.
'Well,' he replied, 'sometimes she's better and sometimes she's worse. But from the way she carries on when she's better, I think she's better when she's worse.'

* * *

Pat was anxiously awaiting a love letter from Bridget so he went to the post office and asked the clerk if there were any letters for him.
'I'll go and see sir,' said the clerk, 'what is your name?'
'You're having me on now,' smiled Pat, 'won't you see it on the envelope?'

* * *

Pat's proposal to Bridget: 'How would you like to be buried with my people?'

* * *

A harmless little film was doing the rounds of the country towns. One particular scene showed a shapely young lady changing her clothes, but just as the scene was becoming exciting a very long train came into view, obscuring her completely. By the time the train had passed, she was fully dressed again.
Pat and Mike followed the film from town to town until they must have seen it at least twenty times. 'It can't be long now,' said Pat, 'some night that train is going to be late.'

* * *

PAT'S LOVE LETTER TO BRIDGET

My Darling Bridget,

I met you last night and you never came. Next time I'll meet you again whether you come or not. If I am there first, I'll write my name on the gatepost to let you know; and if it's you that's first rub out my name and nobody will be the wiser.

Darling Bridget, I would climb the highest mountain for your sake, and swim the widest sea. I would endure any hardship and suffer any trial to spend a moment by your side.

Your own ever loving

Pat

P.S. I'll be over to see you on Friday night if it's not raining.

* * *

After an uneventful ten year courtship Bridget said, 'Pat, don't you think it's time we were getting married?'
'Don't be a fool woman,' said Pat, 'shure who would marry either of us at this stage of our lives?'

* * *

Pat and Bridget were having trouble with their marriage so they decided to go and see a marriage counsellor. The counsellor decided that Pat was not sufficiently aware of the female anatomy to satisfy his wife Bridget.
'For example,' the counsellor asked Pat, 'do you know where the clitoris is?'
'Is it near Mullingar?' said Pat.

* * *

While they were courting, Pat was explaining the mysteries of Nature to his beloved Bridget.
'Why are the days long in Summer and short in Winter?' Bridget asked.
'Heat expands and cold contracts, my love,' explained Pat.

* * *

96

'Mike is the meanest man in the world,' said a girl to Bridget.
'Why do you say that?' asked Bridget.
'Well,' said the girl,'I've decided to refuse him if he proposes to me, and the mean old so-and-so won't propose.'

* * *

Bridget's father:	'Do you think you could support my daughter if you married her?'
Pat:	'Yes, sir.'
Bridget's father:	'Have you ever seen her eat?'
Pat:	'Yes, sir.'
Bridget's father:	'Have you ever seen her eat when there's nobody looking?'

* * *

Pat died leaving his widow Bridget over £50,000. The lawyers however, took months and months to settle the estate and Bridget was getting fed up with all the red tape and technicalities she had to wade through.
'Sometimes,' she confided in a friend, 'I'm sorry Pat ever died. Do you know I'd give £10,000 of that money just to have him back again.'

* * *

'A wife,' claimed Mike, is someone who will share with you all the troubles you wouldn't have had in the first place if you hadn't married her.'

* * *

When Pat died a friend consoled Bridget by saying that at least from now on she wouldn't have to wonder where he was at night.

* * *

Bridget:	'Pat, let us go somewhere so that we can be alone together.'
Pat:	'Right, Bridget, and afterwards we'll meet back here.'

* * *

13

RED RAGS TO A BULL – CLOTHES HORSES

The Irish have always worn clothes, even when they were naked savages without a stitch on their backs. In fact, in ancient Ireland, the clothes a man wore signified his social station. Women too, dressed according to their marital status, and their gay and colourful outfits added a splash of interest to otherwise drab lives. Because clothes and footwear were important items in a cold climate, naturally they were talked about, and when they were talked about, bulls and blunders arose. Here are a few of them.

* * *

Pat didn't hold with nudists. 'If God had meant us to be nudists,' he used to say, 'we would have been born with no clothes on.'

* * *

Mike was looking for his hat and asked Pat to help him.
'Why it's on your head all the time,' he told him.
'Thank you,' said Mike, 'If it wasn't for you I would have gone home without it.'

* * *

Bridget had a blanket that was too short, so she cut several strips off the bottom and sewed them on the top.

* * *

Sign in a shop:
Trousers £5 a pair – they won't last long at this price

* * *

Pat was asked in a quiz why mohair was so expensive. He said it was because the mo was such a rare animal.

* * *

Mike always had trouble with his footwear. He used to say that he never could get into his shoes until he had worn them for a few days.

* * *

From an Irish magazine advertisement:
These belts will last for ever and afterwards they can be used for luggage.

* * *

'Is this your cap I've just found?' said Pat to Mike.
'No Pat, ' replied Mike, 'It looks like mine but it can't be mine because mine is lost.'

* * *

Bridget bought a new £500 wool suit for Pat as a present but when she brought it home she was disgusted to find that it had a label saying '100% cotton'. She took it back to the shop and complained.
'Don't be alarmed, madam,' said the man in the shop, 'it's merely a device to fool the moths.'

* * *

Mike claimed he had a belt with only one end because he had cut the other end off.

* * *

Pat met Mike with his overcoat buttoned up on a hot day.
'Why are you dressed like that?' he asked him.
Mike replied, 'it's to hide the shirt I haven't got on.'

* * *

Bridget announced to the family that she had just bought a new pair of waterproof gloves. 'Now,' she boasted, 'I can wash my hands without getting them wet.'

* * *

Pat was very ingenious in disguising his lack of an extensive wardrobe. For example, he always turned his stockings inside out when there was a hole in the other side.

* * *

Mike was parading down the main street wearing one brown shoe and one black shoe.
'That's a mighty unusual pair of shoes you're wearing, Mike,' Bridget remarked to him.
'Not at all,' retorted Mike, 'I've got another pair at home exactly like them.'

* * *

Pat and Mike were passing a nudist colony which was surrounded by a high wall, so Pat stood on Mike's shoulders to have a look inside.
'Are they men or women?' Mike asked from underneath.
'I can't tell,' said Pat, 'they haven't got any clothes on.'

* * *

Bridget went into a large clothing store to buy a cap for her husband Pat. Over an hour later she left the store in despair because she couldn't find one with a peak at the back.

* * *

Mike's shoe size is eight but he always wears nines because he finds that eights are a bit too tight for him.

* * *

Pat went into a shoe shop and came out carrying a pair of wellington boots. An hour later he was back asking for a pair tied together with a shorter piece of string.

* * *

'That fellow is so dishonest,' said Mike of a friend, 'that if he was dropped on a desert island, he would go round stealing money out of the pockets of the penniless and naked savages.'

* * *

Bridget was asked what she thought of a certain shopkeeper. 'That fellow is so crooked,' she observed, 'that half the wool he pulls over your eyes is cotton.'

* * *

Bridget was having great difficulty with the buttons on her new dress. She complained that she never had a dress that buttoned behind before.

* * *

Mike's wife had an old vacuum cleaner that was beyond repair, so she asked him to take it into the junk shop so he might get a few pounds for it.
She commented, 'It's better than having it lying around gathering dust.'

* * *

Pat was shopping in the city and saw a £1,000 toupee of luxuriant hair in a shop window.
'Isn't it amazing,' he said to Bridget, 'how they can make hair grow on that thing but not on your head.'

* * *

Bridget's shoes smelled something terrible but she decided to put up with them rather than choke to death on an odoreater.

* * *

Bridget couldn't understand why environmentalists made such a fuss about sealskin coats because her sealskin coat had come from a dead seal.

* * *

14

PAPAL BULLS, HOLY COWS AND PARABULLS—
RELIGION

Religion has always been a strong feature of Irish life and the metaphysical nature of this subject gives rise to a great number of bulls and blunders. The earthly limitations of language are exposed when we begin to discuss divine subjects, eternal and infernal. We will see that Irish bulls are to be found in the Bible and that the sermons and utterances of great religious leaders are not always free from the influence of the Taurus Hibernicus. A famous Northern Irish Bull was perpetrated when it was seriously proposed that Catholics and Protestants should get together to get rid of ecumenism!

*　　*　　*

The slogan of the Irish atheist is world-famous — Thank God I'm an atheist.

*　　*　　*

Pat decided to become an atheist and one day he was heard to remark, 'I wonder if God knows I'm an atheist? I wish to God I could believe in God.'

*　　*　　*

Mike was telling a joke about a man who received a letter which said 'if you can't read this note, take it to the parish priest and he will read it for you.'
'I get it,' laughed Bridget, 'what if the parish priest was out when he arrived with the letter?'

*　　*　　*

The first time that Bridget met a married Protestant clergy-man with a family she was scandalised.

'Calls himself father,' she said indignantly, 'and him with four children.'

* * *

'Tell me,' said Pat to the bishop, 'is God all-powerful?'

'He is that, Pat,' said the bishop, sipping his pint.

'Well tell me,' said Pat, 'could he make a stone so heavy he couldn't lift it?'

'He could,' said the bishop, 'and then, just to prove he was all-powerful, he would go and lift it.'

* * *

One of the best papal bulls on record concerns the Vatican's Index of Forbidden books. The Index proved such popular reading with those seeking improper reading material, that in the next edition the Index itself was included in the Index!

* * *

Mike was on his deathbed so he told his wife to send for the Minister because he wanted to become a Protestant.

'Why Mike,' asked his wife, 'when you have been a staunch Catholic all your life?'

'I'd much prefer,' groaned Mike, 'to see one of them so-and-so's going rather than one of us.'

* * *

'Isn't one man as good as another?' the priest said to Pat.

'He is, father,' agreed Pat, 'and a great deal better.'

* * *

Bridget was upset by the way people rushed for the doors of the church the very moment proceedings were finished.

'There would be no problem,' she said, 'if they all sat quietly in their places like me until the crush had gone.'

* * *

Mike in a fit of religious enthusiasm decided to become a Muslim. 'There is no God,' he used to say, 'and I am his prophet.'

* * *

Pat was complimenting the priest after a particularly fine piece of preaching.
'That sermon father,' he said to him, 'was like a drink of water to a drowning man.'

* * *

Bridget was explaining the Christmas story to one of her children. Showing him a picture in an illustrated bible, she said, 'And this is where the baby Jesus was born on the first Christmas Eve.'

* * *

The following advertisement is said to have appeared in a Northern Irish Newspaper:
'Man and woman wanted to milk two cows, both protestant.'

* * *

Mike was leading the evening prayers in his household. He intoned, 'let us now pray for people in uninhabited areas of the world.'

* * *

'Did you go to see the Pope when he visited Ireland?' Bridget asked a friend.
'No,' said the friend.
'What a pity,' said Bridget, 'if only you had been there to see how wonderful it was, you would have been sorry to have missed it.'

* * *

A Belfast widow was describing her Orange husband's last few minutes on earth. 'First of all,' she wept, 'he asked for his wee sash, and then he asked for his wee fife. Then he asked for his wee drum, and shouting *To hell with the pope*, he flew straight into the arms of Jesus.'

* * *

'Everyman,' declared Pat, 'should have freedom of conscience and behaviour, and those that don't want to should be forced to.'

* * *

Bridget was consoling a neighbour whose husband had died. 'I'm sorry to hear that your husband is gone to heaven,' she told her, 'and that his friends and relatives will never see him again.'

* * *

Mike's son went to England and got a job in a crematorium. He wrote home to say that he was having the time of his life — burning Protestants and getting paid for it.

* * *

Pat was continually complaining despite the fact that he was in a state of perfect health.
'You ungrateful fellow,' said his more religious wife Bridget, 'get on your knees and thank God you are still on your feet.'

* * *

Mike was fed up with all the morbid sermons about death that he kept hearing in Church.
'Death,' he declared, 'is something we can all live without.'

* * *

Irish bulls have penetrated right into the bible itself. In the Book of Isaiah, chapter 37, verse 36, we read —

'Then the angel of the Lord went forth, and smote in the camp of the Assyrians a hundred and four score and five thousand: and when they arose early in the morning, behold, they were all dead corpses.'

In the New Testament we read:
'And he said "saddle me an ass," so they saddled him.'

* * *

Pat's five year old little boy, who was a Catholic, was staying with some Protestant friends. One evening the woman of the house gave him a bath which he shared with a little four year old girl. When he returned home he said to his father, 'I never knew there was such a difference between Catholics and Protestants.'

* * *

Mike declared that the Lord God was not a lover of newspapers.
'He was born on Christmas Day, and he died on Good Friday', he declared, 'the two days the papers aren't published.'

* * *

15

BULLS IN LABOUR – WORK

Work is a four letter word in Ireland and the average Irishman likes work so much he can sit down all day watching someone else doing it. There is all the difference in the world between an Irishman looking for a job and looking for work. Traditionally, the Irish in England and the United States have been connected with the building and construction industries and it is from this source that most of the bulls and blunders in this chapter arise.

* * *

Pat applied for a job at the building site and was being interviewed by the foreman. 'It's like this,' he told him. 'I can't give you a start to-day, but if you come back tomorrow I might have something for you. The position is that I have a fellow here to-day who hasn't turned up for work. If he doesn't come again tomorrow, I'll send him home, and you can have his job.'

* * *

Mike got a job on a building site and one of the first things he saw was the following notice:
HOLES PAINTED WHITE ARE NOT TO BE DRILLED

* * *

Bridget read the following household hint in a magazine: 'Grease stains on clothes may be removed with ammonia, but old stains, being hard to remove, must be treated as soon as they are made.'

* * *

Pat and Mike were working on a building site.

'Have you the hammer Mike?' asked Pat.

'I have, Pat,' replied Mike.

'Where have you it?' said Pat.

'I have it lost,' said Mike.

* * *

Pat met Mike carrying a door under his arm.

'I've lost the key,' explained Mike, 'and I'm carrying this door in case anybody breaks into the house.'

'But what if you lose the door?' asked Pat.

'Don't worry,' said Mike, 'I've left a window open.'

* * *

Pat and Mike were building a house together but Pat kept throwing away all the nails.

'Why are you doing that?' Mike asked him.

'These nails are defective,' said Pat, the heads are on the wrong end.'

'You fool,' said Mike, 'those are for the other side of the house.'

* * *

Bridget was a do-it-yourself enthusiast so she bought a household ladder that was advertised as follows. This ladder will last forever if you don't wear out the rungs with use.

* * *

'They're not building houses like they used to,' maintained Pat, 'show me any modern building that has lasted as long as the old ones.'

* * *

Mike had an axe that he had inherited from his great grandfather and it had been in continuous use in his family for over a hundred years. In that time it had only five new heads and six new handles.

* * *

Pat applied for a job on a building site and told the foreman he had forty years experience.

'How old are you?' asked the foreman.

'Thirty-five,' replied Pat.

'How do you explain that then?' asked the foreman.

'I did a lot of overtime,' said Pat.

* * *

A town council in Ireland once passed the following resolution.

1. Resolved	That a new jail be built.
2. Resolved:	That the materials of the old jail be used in the construction of the new jail.
3. Resolved:	That the old jail remain in use until the new jail is opened.

* * *

Pat got a job on a building site but he got the sack because he left without giving notice.

* * *

Mike bemoaned the fact that Ireland once had a leaning tower which deviated from the perpendicular even more than the famous tower of Pisa, but some genius straightened it.

* * *

Bridget was rushing round her kitchen with a paint brush sloshing paint all over the walls. She was trying to finish the job before all the paint ran out.

* * *

Pat and Mike joined the local fire brigade and one night they were called to quell a big fire. As they poured water on the flames, Pat said 'Take it easy a bit Mike and let it burn up so we can see what we are doing.'

* * *

Pat had built a barn for his donkey but found that the donkey refused to go in because its ears were catching on the top of the doorway. When Bridget suggested that he should dig a little trench along the doorway Pat retorted, 'Don't be stupid woman, it's the donkey's ears that are causing the problem, not his feet.'

* * *

Pat and Mike were working on a building site and Pat was heard to call out to his workmate, 'Don't come down that ladder, Mike, I've taken it away.'

* * *

Pat: 'Where is the hammer, Mike?'
Mike: 'It's lost, Pat.'
Pat: 'If you don't find it I'll knock the brains out of your empty skull with it.'

* * *

Pat and Mike were trying to finish a job on a dark night.
Pat: 'Have you a light there Mike?'
Mike: 'I have, Pat, but it's gone out.'

* * *

Bridget's doorbell was broken so she sent for an electrician. A week later she rang him to ask why he hadn't called. 'I called three times,' he told her, 'but nobody answered the bell.'

* * *

Pat and Mike were way behind schedule on a building job so they decided to increase their work rate.
'We'll finish this house this morning,' declared Pat, 'even if it takes us all day to do so.'

* * *

Mike lived all his life near a church and every hour on the hour the bell rang. One night he went to sleep at midnight and at 1 a.m. the bell failed to ring. Mike sat bolt upright in his bed and said, 'What was that?'

* * *

Pat and Mike were painting a house and Mike was working on a high ladder painting an upstairs window.
'Have you a good grip on that paintbrush, Mike?' asked Pat.
'I have indeed, Pat,' replied Mike.
'Then hold on tight,' said Pat, 'because I'm taking the ladder away.'

* * *

The great lexicographer Samuel Johnson must have lived in an Irish bullding because in his famous dictionary he defined the attic as the highest room in the house, and the garret as the room above the attic.

* * *

Bridget returned home to find that some joker had sealed up the keyhole of her front door and painted it over.
'Whoever stole my keyhole,' she commented, 'it won't do him much good, because I've got the key in my pocket.'

* * *

Irish newspaper report: 'The fire was put out before any damage could be caused by the local fire brigade.'

* * *

Mike had been killed on the building site when a steam-hammer fell from a great height and hit him on the chest.
'I'm not surprised,' said Bridget, 'Mike always had a weak chest.'

* * *

Bridget was attending a lecture on archaeology at her local college. 'Look at the great cities of antiquity,' thundered the lecturer, 'some of them have vanished so utterly that it is doubtful whether they ever existed at all.'

* * *

Pat was working on a building site and the foreman asked him to dispose of some rubble, so Pat dug a hole.
'Now where are you going to put the dirt from the hole?' asked the foreman.
'I'll dig another hole,' said Pat,
'How will that help?' asked the foreman again.
'I'll dig the other hole deeper,' said Pat.

* * *

Finally, a Russian Bull from the great Lenin, 'Liberty', he used to say, 'is the most precious thing in the world. It is so precious that it has to be strictly rationed'.

* * *

16

A FEW ODD BULLS
THE TALE END OF THE BULL

During a long hot summer there was a sudden rainstorm. Pat remarked, 'An hour of this rain will do as much good in ten minutes as a month of it would do in a fortnight at any other time of the year.'

* * *

Mike was at a concert given by a world famous blind pianist. 'It wouldn't matter if he wasn't blind,' said Mike, 'because I watched him all the time and he never looked at the piano once.'

* * *

Pat and Bridget once stayed at a hotel but they weren't very satisfied with the service. When they left they entered the following complaints in the visitors book:

1. The hot water in the bathroom was always cold.
2. There were no handles on the taps except one that was broken off.
3. The daily newspapers were not available and the light was so poor we couldn't read them.
4. The food was terrible and the portions were too small.

* * *

Mike's lad Sean was asked to write an essay about his favourite bird. He chose the cuckoo and began as follows, 'The cuckoo is an unusual bird. He doesn't lay his own eggs and he lives in a clock.'

* * *

Bridget is not superstitious – she's afraid it might bring her bad luck.

* * *

Pat was explaining to Bridget the difficulties of making contact with the inhabitants of the planets and stars.
'We will never be able to communicate with the beings of outer space,' he told her, 'until we can first notify them with a signal to be on the lookout for a communication.'

* * *

Mike was speaking on a political platform in a large hall.
'Can all you people at the back of the hall hear me?' he shouted.
'No, we can't', they shouted back.

* * *

Pat's cigarette lighter was broken but he fixed it up fine. Now he can use it by lighting two matches.

* * *

Mike was in the big city without a watch so he asked a passing man for the time.
'It's half past two,' replied the man, 'That's funny,' said Mike 'I've been asking people that all day, and getting different answers, and to prove it, I've written them all down on this piece of paper.'

* * *

Pat and Mike were taking part in a big card game and Pat was dealing.
'Hold on a moment,' shouted Mike, 'there's a pound missing from the pot – who put it in?'

* * *

Pat was doing some repairs to his house when a brick fell from a great height and hit him on the eye. As he recovered consciousness, his wife Bridget tenderly asked him, 'can you see at all with the eye that's knocked out?'

* * *

Notice in a newspaper — because of lack of space, several births have been postponed until next week.

* * *

Declared Bridget, 'Ireland used to be a very ancient country but with all the new buildings things have changed out of all recognition in the recent past.'

* * *

Pat received a new toolkit and on comparing it with the invoice found that it contained everything except a chisel which was missing, so he took it back to the shop.
'I have it here,' said the shopkeeper, 'I just took it out to open the case with it.'

* * *

Mike was giving evidence in a court case. 'I questioned the defendant, your honour, ' he told the judge, 'and he admitted to being deaf and dumb.'

* * *

From a newspaper report: 'After a fruitless search, all the money was recovered except for a pearl necklace.

* * *

Pat was annoyed because he had not been asked to deliver the oration at the funeral of a friend.
'If the dead man was asked at this moment who he wanted to speak,' he declared, 'I'm sure it's me he would choose.'

* * *

Newspaper Report: Because of bad weather the sun was not visible in Ireland during its recent total eclipse.'

* * *

According to the Dubliners, the Irish Navy is the only navy on Earth where all the sailors go home for their tea.

* * *

In certain Irish schools it is customary to cane the last two pupils who arrive for classes each day.

* * *

Mike always had difficulty reading the morning newspaper because he was educated at night school.

* * *

Mike got his rates bill from the County Council and it had a £25 charge for sewage, so he stormed round to the Council and told them that he hadn't received any sewage from them. 'We called to deliver it but you were not in,' said the official. 'Couldn't you have put it through the letterbox?' said Mike.

* * *

Pat was out walking one day when he saw a sign
            REFUSE TO BE PUT IN THIS LITTER BIN.
Pat got into the bin saying 'Nobody tells me what to do in my own country.'

* * *

Bridget was reading *The Cork Examiner*. 'Isn't it amazing,' she said to Pat, 'how just enough things seem to happen every day to fill the newspaper.'

* * *

Mike heard that by putting a brick in your toilet cistern you could conserve water. So he put a brick in his petrol tank.

* * *

Pat was in a philosophical mood. 'When one counts the accidents, dangers and diseases which beset us on our journey through life,' he declared, 'it's amazing that so many people live until they die.'

*　　*　　*

Mike was looking at a photograph of his ancestral home. 'That is the house,' he said proudly, 'that my father built and my grandfather was born in.'

*　　*　　*

Bridget was giving an account of a boating accident.
'One poor fellow,' she said, 'couldn't be saved until after he was drowned.'

*　　*　　*

Pat was about to buy a new house for Bridget but she complained that the front door was at the side.

*　　*　　*

Mike was the caretaker of a building that was on fire.
'Let me in, let me in,' said a brash young reporter, 'I represent the press and I've come to report on the fire.'
'Go home,' said Mike, 'you can read all about it in the papers in the morning.'

*　　*　　*

Pat sent the following reply to his shoemaker: 'I never ordered those shoes, and if I did, you never sent them, and if you did, I never got them, and if I did, I paid for them, and if I didn't, I won't.'

*　　*　　*

Pat was talking about his visit to the Vatican. He told his listeners that it is a Mecca for tourists.

*　　*　　*

When Maria Edgeworth wrote her famous *Irish Bulls* a copy was ordered by the Scottish Cattle Breeding Association who were most disappointed with the contents.

*   *   *

Finally, an absolutely authentic Irish Bull about the three stallions bought by the Irish Government, a tail uncovered a mare month after this book was published. The first stallion was found to be infertile. The second stallion was found to have only one testicle. And the third stallion was completely ineffective because of a wheezy chest which afflicted him in moments of excitement!!!

*   *   *

Humorous Quotations

Des MacHale

Do you know who said:

'I always arrive late at the office, but make up for it by leaving early'.

'I wish dear Karl could have spent some time acquiring capital instead of merely writing about it'.

'Work is the curse of the drinking classes'.

'When I came back to Dublin I was court-martialled in my absence and sentenced to death in my absence, so I said they could shoot me in my absence'.

'Insanity is hereditary; you can get it from your children'.

'He who throws mud loses ground'.

Dictionary of Irish Quotations

Sean Sheehan

Dictionary of Irish Quotations contains a highly enjoyable and varied selection of interesting, informative, intriguing, infuriating – and sometimes just witty – remarks by Irish people on a number of topical subjects. There are over 150 authors – from St Brigid to Sinéad O'Connor. Yeats and Swift are quoted here and Wilde and Joyce. So too are Robert Emmet, Douglas Hyde, Mary Robinson, Sean Hughes, Neil Jordan ...